JUMBLE
Time Machine: 1993

A collection of puzzles from 30 years ago!

Henri Arnold,
Bob Lee,
and
Michael Argirion

TRIUMPH
B O O K S

For further information, con tact:
Triumph Books LLC
814 North Franklin Street
Chicago, Illinois 60610
Phone: (312) 337-0747
www.triumphbooks.com

Printed in U.S.A.

ISBN: 978-1-63727-293-0

Design by Sue Knopf

Contents

JUMBLE®

TIME MACHINE: 1993

Classic Puzzles

Unscramble these four Jumbles, one letter
to each square, to form four ordinary words.

AMMIX

NIDEK

TRAISE

VEEDIC

WHAT THE TERRIBLE-
TEMPERED SUGAR
GROWER DID.

Now arrange the circled letters
to form the surprise answer, as
suggested by the above cartoon.

Print answer here

JUMBLE®

Unscramble these four Jumbles, one letter
to each square, to form four ordinary words.

GLEEY

OTTOH

ROCTAV

SUNDAI

Wow! 100%
in math!

Extra
credit
for
neatness

A PERSON WHO
MAKES LITTLE
THINGS COUNT.

Now arrange the circled letters
to form the surprise answer, as
suggested by the above cartoon.

Print answer here A ⬡⬡⬡⬡⬡⬡⬡

JUMBLE.

Unscramble these four Jumbles, one letter
to each square, to form four ordinary words.

DESET

TRAIE

NERUNG

WARMOR

Hey — wanna
get killed?!

SCREECH!

WHAT JAYWALKERS
MAY BE WEARING
TOMORROW.

Now arrange the circled letters
to form the surprise answer, as
suggested by the above cartoon.

Print answer here

JUMBLE®

Unscramble these four Jumbles, one letter
to each square, to form four ordinary words.

GNAAP

YWDDO

CEDBEK

WURFOR

That does it!!

WHAT A FEW
CATTY REMARKS
TURNED THE LADIES'
LOUNGE INTO.

Now arrange the circled letters
to form the surprise answer, as
suggested by the above cartoon.

Print answer here A ⬡⬡⬡⬡⬡⬡ ⬡⬡⬡

JUMBLE

Unscramble these four Jumbles, one letter to each square, to form four ordinary words.

ANCOP

DRAIP

MUDINS

LEMITY

Sure loves himself

WHAT THE EGOTIST WAS SUFFERING FROM.

Now arrange the circled letters to form the surprise answer, as suggested by the above cartoon.

Print answer here " ☐ " ☐☐☐☐☐☐☐

JUMBLE®

Unscramble these four Jumbles, one letter
to each square, to form four ordinary words.

SYKAH

RODAH

IMVOTE

STEJER

WHAT THE CUTE
LITTLE POTATO WAS
WARNED AGAINST.

Now arrange the circled letters
to form the surprise answer, as
suggested by the above cartoon.

Print answer here

JUMBLE®

Unscramble these four Jumbles, one letter to each square, to form four ordinary words.

YONIR

TOJUS

YONIFT

WURCEF

WHAT THE CHIROPRACTOR AND HIS WIFE WERE WORKING ON.

Now arrange the circled letters to form the surprise answer, as suggested by the above cartoon.

Print answer here A

Unscramble these four Jumbles, one letter
to each square, to form four ordinary words.

SOMYS

RUGPO

GORUME

THEIRE

WHAT BOARDING
HOUSE GOSSIP USED
TO START WITH.

Now arrange the circled letters
to form the surprise answer, as
suggested by the above cartoon.

Print answer here " ⬡⬡⬡⬡⬡⬡⬡ "

9

JUMBLE®

Unscramble these four Jumbles, one letter
to each square, to form four ordinary words.

ASOBS

MORRA

KALTEC

CUSTOC

WHAT THE
TWELVE BOTTLES OF
MOONSHINE EVENTUALLY
BECAME.

Now arrange the circled letters
to form the surprise answer, as
suggested by the above cartoon.

Print answer here A

JUMBLE

Unscramble these four Jumbles, one letter
to each square, to form four ordinary words.

STYTA

MIRPE

HUNGOE

DESAUB

Now arrange the circled letters
to form the surprise answer, as
suggested by the above cartoon.

Print answer here " ⬡⬡ ⬡⬡⬡⬡⬡ "

Unscramble these four Jumbles, one letter
to each square, to form four ordinary words.

GUFED

SIVAT

CUDLAN

CEETIN

RATHER BIG
FOR BALLET
THESE DAYS.

Now arrange the circled letters
to form the surprise answer, as
suggested by the above cartoon.

Print answer here

JUMBLE®

Unscramble these four Jumbles, one letter
to each square, to form four ordinary words.

TUMON

FLYIM

FRINIM

YAXLAG

Your
steak,
sir

WHAT HORSEMEAT
IS TO A DOG.

Now arrange the circled letters
to form the surprise answer, as
suggested by the above cartoon.

Print
answer
here   " ◯◯◯◯◯◯ " ◯◯◯◯◯◯

JUMBLE®

Unscramble these four Jumbles, one letter to each square, to form four ordinary words.

BILLE

BELZA

YAUNES

REMAID

WHAT SHE WAS AFTER POSING FOR A FULL-LENGTH PORTRAIT.

Now arrange the circled letters to form the surprise answer, as suggested by the above cartoon.

Print answer here

JUMBLE.

Unscramble these four Jumbles, one letter
to each square, to form four ordinary words.

AMELY

SUGES

YUPRIF

INLATE

WE CLOSE OUR
EYES TO THIS.

Now arrange the circled letters
to form the surprise answer, as
suggested by the above cartoon.

Print answer here

JUMBLE®

Unscramble these four Jumbles, one letter
to each square, to form four ordinary words.

PLIMB

BYBOH

ENBLIM

GRANDO

Stand still!

WHERE THE OVER-
ZEALOUS COW
GAVE HER MILK.

Now arrange the circled letters
to form the surprise answer, as
suggested by the above cartoon.

Print
answer
here

◯◯◯◯◯◯ THE " ◯◯◯◯ "

JUMBLE®

Unscramble these four Jumbles, one letter to each square, to form four ordinary words.

SEERA

PUTIL

DIRTOR

VIRQUE

WHAT THE
PRISON DESIGNER
CREATED.

Now arrange the circled letters to form the surprise answer, as suggested by the above cartoon.

Print answer here

Unscramble these four Jumbles, one letter
to each square, to form four ordinary words.

BAITH

AMDAM

GRATUI

LAMORF

Don't forget
the ketchup

SOMEONE WHO RAIDS
THE REFRIGERATOR
FOR A MIDNIGHT
SNACK.

Now arrange the circled letters
to form the surprise answer, as
suggested by the above cartoon.

Print
answer A "◯◯◯ - ◯◯◯◯◯◯◯"
here

JUMBLE®

Unscramble these four Jumbles, one letter
to each square, to form four ordinary words.

GLOIN

NUWDE

MIRTHE

YORCAN

IT'S USUAL TO
HAVE THIS BEFORE
DINNER.

Now arrange the circled letters
to form the surprise answer, as
suggested by the above cartoon.

Print answer here

JUMBLE

Unscramble these four Jumbles, one letter
to each square, to form four ordinary words.

GANOW

PUBYM

SEATTL

RANLEY

WHAT HIS OLD
FLAME DID WHEN
SHE SAW HIM WITH
ANOTHER GIRL.

Now arrange the circled letters
to form the surprise answer, as
suggested by the above cartoon.

Print answer here A ☐☐☐☐☐ ☐☐☐☐☐

JUMBLE®

Unscramble these four Jumbles, one letter to each square, to form four ordinary words.

EWLEH

REMEB

IBINIK

RANLYX

See ya around

WHAT THE TRAVELING CORRESPONDENT'S WIFE DIDN'T LIKE.

Now arrange the circled letters to form the surprise answer, as suggested by the above cartoon.

Print answer here HIS " ☐☐☐ ☐☐☐☐ "

JUMBLE®

Unscramble these four Jumbles, one letter to each square, to form four ordinary words.

FRADT

MYTEP

VINTER

GRUEFE

YOU CAN ALWAYS GROW THIS IN YOUR GARDEN IF YOU WORK HARD ENOUGH.

Now arrange the circled letters to form the surprise answer, as suggested by the above cartoon.

Print answer here

JUMBLE

Unscramble these four Jumbles, one letter
to each square, to form four ordinary words.

MAWPS

MEPOT

LETHAH

FERPER

Food's great here

But not much ambience

WHAT THE
RESTAURANT ON
THE MOON LACKED.

Now arrange the circled letters
to form the surprise answer, as
suggested by the above cartoon.

Print answer here

JUMBLE®

Unscramble these four Jumbles, one letter
to each square, to form four ordinary words.

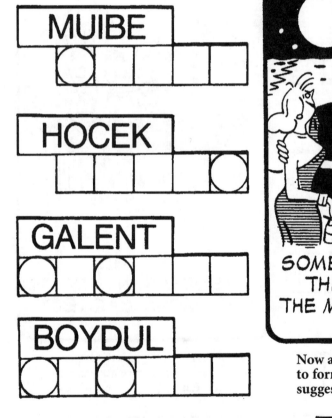

MUIBE

HOCEK

GALENT

BOYDUL

SOMETHING BESIDES
THE TIDE WHICH
THE MOON AFFECTS.

Now arrange the circled letters
to form the surprise answer, as
suggested by the above cartoon.

Print answer here   THE ⬡⬡⬡⬡⬡⬡

JUMBLE®

Unscramble these four Jumbles, one letter to each square, to form four ordinary words.

WROCE

PUJEL

BLITAR

MAINEA

HAIRCUT $40
SHAVE $20
SHAMPOO $30

WHAT YOU MIGHT CALL THIS BARBER'S ESTABLISHMENT.

Now arrange the circled letters to form the surprise answer, as suggested by the above cartoon.

Print answer here   A

JUMBLE®

Unscramble these four Jumbles, one letter to each square, to form four ordinary words.

YAHND

DUGAY

FEANED

DUSAIR

WHAT DID THE EXUBERANT WIFE DO WHEN HER HUSBAND STRUCK OIL?

Now arrange the circled letters to form the surprise answer, as suggested by the above cartoon.

Print answer here   SHE

JUMBLE

TIME MACHINE: 1993

Daily Puzzles

JUMBLE®

Unscramble these four Jumbles, one letter
to each square, to form four ordinary words.

DEROO

VORAF

HYRITT

LIRBED

The world's
gone to pot

The end can't
be far off

WHAT SHE CALLED
HER SOURPUSS
HUSBAND.

Now arrange the circled letters
to form the surprise answer, as
suggested by the above cartoon.

*Print answer
here*   HER

JUMBLE®

Unscramble these four Jumbles, one letter
to each square, to form four ordinary words.

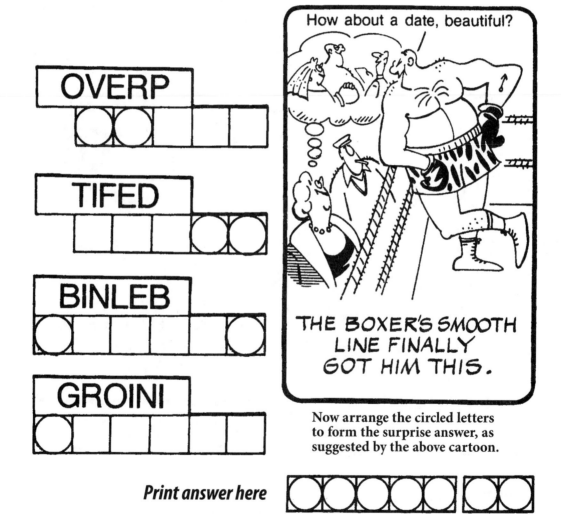

How about a date, beautiful?

THE BOXER'S SMOOTH
LINE FINALLY
GOT HIM THIS.

OVERP

TIFED

BINLEB

GROINI

Now arrange the circled letters
to form the surprise answer, as
suggested by the above cartoon.

Print answer here

JUMBLE®

Unscramble these four Jumbles, one letter to each square, to form four ordinary words.

ROGAC

FINEK

TIPPEC

TINKTE

A MAN WHOSE WORK REQUIRES HIM TO GRASP THINGS QUICKLY.

Now arrange the circled letters to form the surprise answer, as suggested by the above cartoon.

Print answer here A ⬡⬡⬡⬡⬡⬡⬡⬡⬡⬡⬡⬡

JUMBLE®

Unscramble these four Jumbles, one letter to each square, to form four ordinary words.

ROGOM

MYOFA

UNCANE

SELING

WHAT HER EARNINGS OFTEN DON'T KEEP UP WITH.

Now arrange the circled letters to form the surprise answer, as suggested by the above cartoon.

Print answer here HER ⬡⬡⬡⬡⬡⬡⬡⬡⬡⬡

Unscramble these four Jumbles, one letter to each square, to form four ordinary words.

VALIE

FONTE

REDDEG

UMSCAP

WHAT THE SAILOR
BECAME WHEN HE
MARRIED A WIDOW.

Now arrange the circled letters
to form the surprise answer, as
suggested by the above cartoon.

Print answer here A ◯◯◯◯◯◯◯ ◯◯◯◯

JUMBLE®

Unscramble these four Jumbles, one letter
to each square, to form four ordinary words.

GLIVI

LIRLT

YIRCKT

WHEPEN

THOSE STORIES
TOLD BY THE
CONSTRUCTION
WORKER WERE---

Now arrange the circled letters
to form the surprise answer, as
suggested by the above cartoon.

Print answer here

Unscramble these four Jumbles, one letter
to each square, to form four ordinary words.

OYLED

AXTEC

PEAQUO

PHYNOT

Oh, Edna--I can't get in

WHAT DO YOU CALL
AN OFFICER WHO
LOST THE KEY
TO HIS HOUSE?

Now arrange the circled letters
to form the surprise answer, as
suggested by the above cartoon.

Print answer here   A "⬡⬡⬡ ⬡⬡⬡"

JUMBLE®

Unscramble these four Jumbles, one letter to each square, to form four ordinary words.

PUPER

HORTT

GAIMBY

UMPING

Say, George--I'm a little short

WHAT HE DID WHEN HE RAN INTO HIS PAL.

Now arrange the circled letters to form the surprise answer, as suggested by the above cartoon.

Print answer here

◯◯◯ THE ◯◯◯◯◯ ON ◯◯◯

JUMBLE®

Unscramble these four Jumbles, one letter
to each square, to form four ordinary words.

NAHVE

IDEPT

DRENGE

YULOHN

They
can
afford
it

PENTHOUSE
DWELLERS USUALLY
PAY THIS.

Now arrange the circled letters
to form the surprise answer, as
suggested by the above cartoon.

Print answer here

JUMBLE®

Unscramble these four Jumbles, one letter
to each square, to form four ordinary words.

VENET

ROFOL

FLUIFT

KENART

ONE OF THE IDEN-
TICAL TWINS WAS
FIVE FEET TALL—
WHAT WAS THE OTHER?

Now arrange the circled letters
to form the surprise answer, as
suggested by the above cartoon.

Print
answer
here

JUMBLE®

Unscramble these four Jumbles, one letter
to each square, to form four ordinary words.

AVUME
☐☐☐◯

RUTYL
◯☐☐☐☐

CEMESH
◯☐◯☐☐☐

DREEME
◯☐☐◯☐☐

Junior wants to go along

PEOPLE IN LOVE
SELDOM TRAVEL
IN THESE.

Now arrange the circled letters
to form the surprise answer, as
suggested by the above cartoon.

Print answer here ◯◯◯◯◯◯◯

PUZZLE
37

JUMBLE®

Unscramble these four Jumbles, one letter
to each square, to form four ordinary words.

USEED

CILLA

TAIROD

YARRIT

WHAT SOME PEOPLE
TRAVEL IN WHILE
REMAINING AT
HOME.

Now arrange the circled letters
to form the surprise answer, as
suggested by the above cartoon.

Print answer here

Unscramble these four Jumbles, one letter
to each square, to form four ordinary words.

SLUPH

MARFE

FESTOF

NATFUL

I can't
get in!

I can't
get out!

THESE ARE STUCK
OUTSIDE AND ALSO
COULD BE STUCK
UNSTUCK INSIDE.

Now arrange the circled letters
to form the surprise answer, as
suggested by the above cartoon.

Print answer here

JUMBLE®

Unscramble these four Jumbles, one letter to each square, to form four ordinary words.

WABLY

UPSIO

RIGLYM

CHORCS

This'll make Page One!

WHAT A CRIME WAVE GETS IN THE NEWSPAPER.

Now arrange the circled letters to form the surprise answer, as suggested by the above cartoon.

Print answer here A ☐☐☐ ☐☐☐☐☐☐

JUMBLE®

Unscramble these four Jumbles, one letter
to each square, to form four ordinary words.

YERNT

TACCH

SITMIF

HEELAX

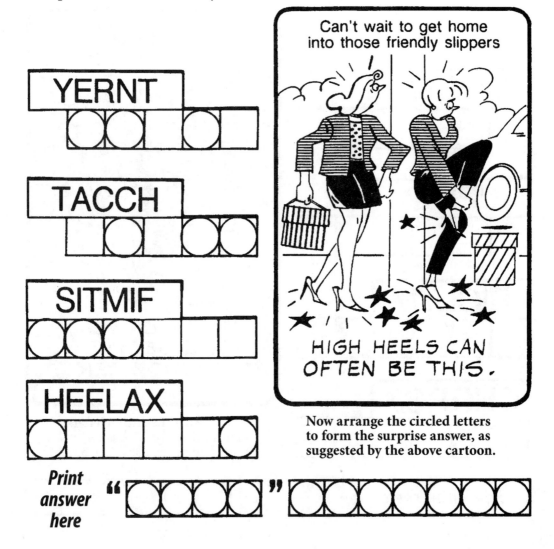

Can't wait to get home
into those friendly slippers

HIGH HEELS CAN
OFTEN BE THIS.

Now arrange the circled letters
to form the surprise answer, as
suggested by the above cartoon.

Print answer here "◯◯◯◯" ◯◯◯◯◯◯◯

JUMBLE®

Unscramble these four Jumbles, one letter
to each square, to form four ordinary words.

KLANF

POSOW

FLAUDE

MOUPID

STAGE
DOOR

IN THE THEATER,
THESE MEAN NO
WORK AND NO PLAY.

Now arrange the circled letters
to form the surprise answer, as
suggested by the above cartoon.

Print answer here

JUMBLE®

Unscramble these four Jumbles, one letter
to each square, to form four ordinary words.

WANTY

CEIPE

UNBOYT

DORWAT

WHAT THE UMPIRE
TURNED PIZZA
CHEF ANNOUNCED.

Now arrange the circled letters
to form the surprise answer, as
suggested by the above cartoon.

Print answer here " ⬡⬡⬡⬡⬡⬡ ⬡⬡ ! "

JUMBLE®

Unscramble these four Jumbles, one letter
to each square, to form four ordinary words.

YITED

TAVIL

FARREY

NEXTTE

HIS BUSINESS
SUCCESS DEPENDS
ON DRIVING
CUSTOMERS AWAY.

Now arrange the circled letters
to form the surprise answer, as
suggested by the above cartoon.

Print answer here A ⬚⬚⬚⬚⬚ ⬚⬚⬚⬚⬚⬚

JUMBLE®

Unscramble these four Jumbles, one letter to each square, to form four ordinary words.

HUVOC

DAGLE

GRATTE

SOARUE

WHAT THE LUMBERJACK WENT DOWNSTREAM ON.

Now arrange the circled letters to form the surprise answer, as suggested by the above cartoon.

Print answer here A "◯◯◯◯◯◯◯◯◯"

JUMBLE®

Unscramble these four Jumbles, one letter
to each square, to form four ordinary words.

LIWLT

AMLET

COASIF

NAHLED

WHAT A DEEP-SEA
DIVER MUST DO
WHEN HE HAS
A PROBLEM.

Now arrange the circled letters
to form the surprise answer, as
suggested by the above cartoon.

Print answer here

JUMBLE®

Unscramble these four Jumbles, one letter
to each square, to form four ordinary words.

WERFE

GLIYN

HERNUT

BOADUN

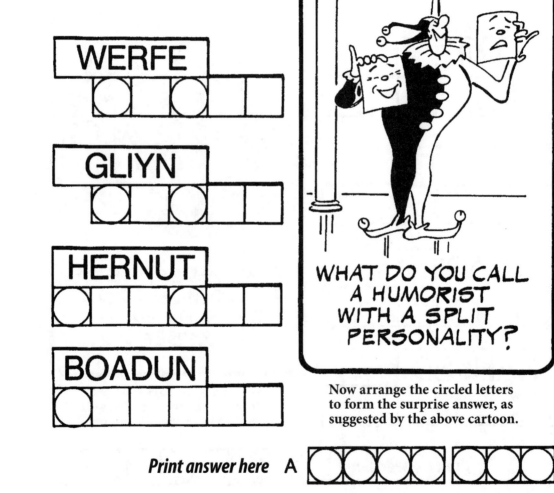

WHAT DO YOU CALL
A HUMORIST
WITH A SPLIT
PERSONALITY?

Now arrange the circled letters
to form the surprise answer, as
suggested by the above cartoon.

Print answer here A ☐☐☐☐☐ ☐☐☐

JUMBLE®

Unscramble these four Jumbles, one letter
to each square, to form four ordinary words.

NEPEC

TURTE

DEBALF

GIFFEY

WHAT THE NEW
OWNER OF THE RUN-
DOWN STEAK HOUSE
TRIED TO DO.

Now arrange the circled letters
to form the surprise answer, as
suggested by the above cartoon.

Print answer here

Unscramble these four Jumbles, one letter
to each square, to form four ordinary words.

We're unique

LIQUA
◯ ◯ □ ◯

CLOIG
□ □ ◯ ◯

RAKNEC
◯ □ □ ◯ □ □

TALCOE
◯ □ ◯ □ □ ◯

WHAT THE CAMERA
CLUB MEMBERS
CALLED THEM-
SELVES.

Now arrange the circled letters
to form the surprise answer, as
suggested by the above cartoon.

**Print
answer
here**

A ◯◯◯◯◯ ◯◯◯◯◯◯

Unscramble these four Jumbles, one letter
to each square, to form four ordinary words.

PEINT

CHELE

GISTED

LUCASE

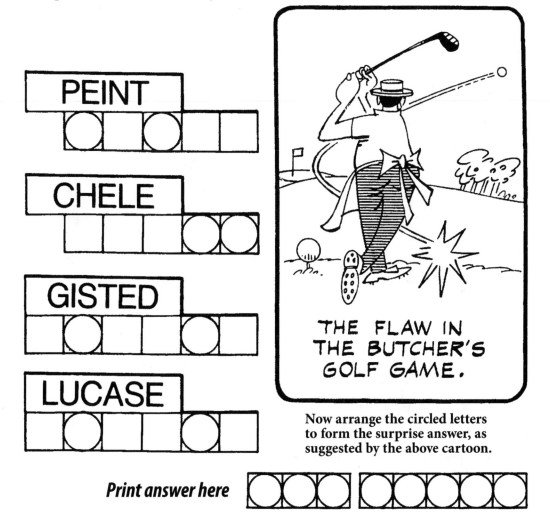

THE FLAW IN
THE BUTCHER'S
GOLF GAME.

Now arrange the circled letters
to form the surprise answer, as
suggested by the above cartoon.

Print answer here

Unscramble these four Jumbles, one letter
to each square, to form four ordinary words.

NOMUD

HECEK

DOMBEY

VEEBAH

HOW THE LAZY
GARDENER FELT
ABOUT HIS WORK.

Now arrange the circled letters
to form the surprise answer, as
suggested by the above cartoon.

Print answer here

JUMBLE®

Unscramble these four Jumbles, one letter
to each square, to form four ordinary words.

TOODU

OPTIA

VINTEN

INFREY

WHAT THE COM-
MERCIAL FISHERMAN
LIVED ON.

Now arrange the circled letters
to form the surprise answer, as
suggested by the above cartoon.

Print answer here

JUMBLE®

Unscramble these four Jumbles, one letter
to each square, to form four ordinary words.

INGAR

FEACH

LEMOTE

ROCCEE

WHAT THE
MELANCHOLY
PAINTER MADE.

Now arrange the circled letters
to form the surprise answer, as
suggested by the above cartoon.

Print answer here

JUMBLE®

Unscramble these four Jumbles, one letter
to each square, to form four ordinary words.

YOLID

SLEBS

QUINUE

NAHZIG

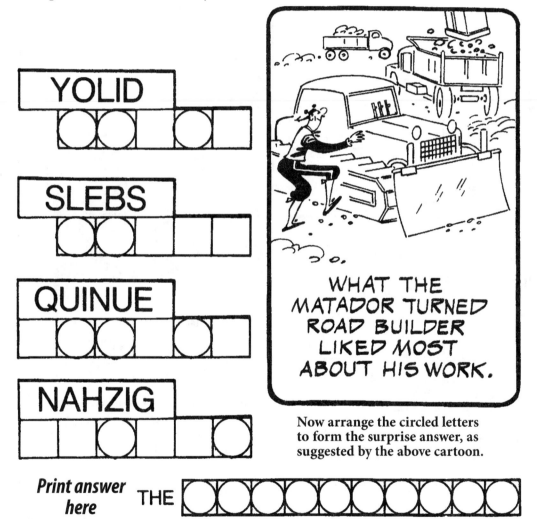

WHAT THE
MATADOR TURNED
ROAD BUILDER
LIKED MOST
ABOUT HIS WORK.

Now arrange the circled letters
to form the surprise answer, as
suggested by the above cartoon.

*Print answer
here* THE ☐☐☐☐☐☐☐☐☐☐

JUMBLE®

Unscramble these four Jumbles, one letter
to each square, to form four ordinary words.

KAYLE

TIPAL

GANDEA

HENBID

THIS CAN TURN
A SHOE INTO
A SLIPPER.

Now arrange the circled letters
to form the surprise answer, as
suggested by the above cartoon.

Print answer
here

A ☐☐☐☐☐☐ ☐☐☐☐

JUMBLE®

Unscramble these four Jumbles, one letter
to each square, to form four ordinary words.

SEMYS
☐☐○○☐

YOWDD
☐○○○☐

DIBITT
○○○☐○○

UNDASE
○○☐○☐○

WHAT THE EPIDEMIC
OF MEASLES IN
GENEVA CREATED.

Now arrange the circled letters
to form the surprise answer, as
suggested by the above cartoon.

Print answer here
○○○○○○ ○○○○○

JUMBLE®

Unscramble these four Jumbles, one letter
to each square, to form four ordinary words.

LUCOT

MALUB

AFDACE

GOHEAM

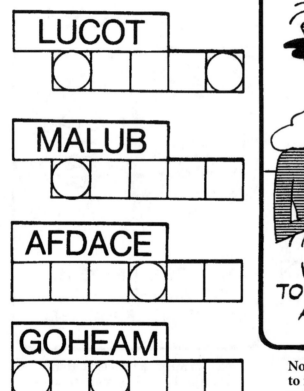

We'll be toasty warm
in here soon

WHAT IT TAKES
TO GET THESE TWO
ALL FIRED UP.

Now arrange the circled letters
to form the surprise answer, as
suggested by the above cartoon.

Print answer here

JUMBLE®

Unscramble these four Jumbles, one letter to each square, to form four ordinary words.

ABNIS

WONNK

CRESPO

GANFIC

WHAT HE WAS AS A RESULT OF TEACHING HIS TEEN-AGER TO DRIVE.

Now arrange the circled letters to form the surprise answer, as suggested by the above cartoon.

Print answer here

JUMBLE®

Unscramble these four Jumbles, one letter
to each square, to form four ordinary words.

STYRT

GRITE

BARNEY

GLINTE

TELLER

WHAT SHE SERVED
THE HANDSOME
DEPOSITOR WITH.

Now arrange the circled letters
to form the surprise answer, as
suggested by the above cartoon.

Print answer here

JUMBLE®

Unscramble these four Jumbles, one letter
to each square, to form four ordinary words.

VALAN

OBOAT

COORTH

WANEDD

WHAT THE
SNOWBALL FIGHT
PROVED TO BE.

Now arrange the circled letters
to form the surprise answer, as
suggested by the above cartoon.

Print answer here A ⟨◯◯◯◯⟩ ⟨◯◯◯⟩

61

JUMBLE®

Unscramble these four Jumbles, one letter
to each square, to form four ordinary words.

ENSOO

ENCIE

TRARAT

VERROF

THE PART OF
THE BOOK THE
PODIATRIST
LIKED BEST.

Now arrange the circled letters
to form the surprise answer, as
suggested by the above cartoon.

Print answer here THE ⬡⬡⬡⬡⬡⬡⬡⬡⬡⬡

JUMBLE®

Unscramble these four Jumbles, one letter to each square, to form four ordinary words.

KNOTE

LEBLE

FRIDAT

DRIFOL

SPORTING GOODS

THE KIND OF GIFT SOME YOUNGSTERS MIGHT KICK ABOUT.

Now arrange the circled letters to form the surprise answer, as suggested by the above cartoon.

Print answer here A ⬡⬡⬡⬡⬡⬡⬡⬡⬡

Unscramble these four Jumbles, one letter
to each square, to form four ordinary words.

NALTS

NORIM

CLAFIA

KERUBE

WHAT THE MATH
GENIUS WITH
SMALL KIDS KNEW
ALL ABOUT.

Now arrange the circled letters
to form the surprise answer, as
suggested by the above cartoon.

Print answer here

1993
PUZZLE
63

JUMBLE®

Unscramble these four Jumbles, one letter
to each square, to form four ordinary words.

FIRGE

ORPYX

AREETA

PRAMCE

WHAT THE TWO
TYCOONS DISCUSSED
AT A LUNCHEON
CONFERENCE.

Now arrange the circled letters
to form the surprise answer, as
suggested by the above cartoon.

Print answer here A

65

Unscramble these four Jumbles, one letter
to each square, to form four ordinary words.

ORDEN
◯◯◯◯◯

IRYAH
◯◯◯◯◯

LOSFIS
◯◯◯◯◯◯

GRACIT
◯◯◯◯◯◯

HOW A CHAMPION -
SHIP RUNNER
MIGHT TAKE A
HIGH HURDLE.

Now arrange the circled letters
to form the surprise answer, as
suggested by the above cartoon.

Print
answer
here
◯◯ ◯◯◯ ◯◯◯◯◯◯◯

JUMBLE®

Unscramble these four Jumbles, one letter
to each square, to form four ordinary words.

AYLIG

CABIS

LABEZA

OXCIBE

WHAT THE
COMPUTER REPAIR-
MAN'S NICKNAME
WAS.

Now arrange the circled letters
to form the surprise answer, as
suggested by the above cartoon.

Print answer here " ◯◯◯ ◯◯◯◯ "

Unscramble these four Jumbles, one letter
to each square, to form four ordinary words.

WENYL

ENWIC

SAWLAY

CLIFEK

A LOW-DOWN
JOINT.

Now arrange the circled letters
to form the surprise answer, as
suggested by the above cartoon.

Print answer here

JUMBLE®

Unscramble these four Jumbles, one letter
to each square, to form four ordinary words.

GUBEN

KULFE

PYGINT

HARPON

THE FIRST THING
YOU PLANT IN
YOUR GARDEN.

Now arrange the circled letters
to form the surprise answer, as
suggested by the above cartoon.

Print answer here

JUMBLE®

Unscramble these four Jumbles, one letter
to each square, to form four ordinary words.

UNFYN

HEGIT

YETTIN

CLIPAD

Psst! Hey Boss...

WHERE YOU MAY
WIND UP IF YOU
LIVE TOO HIGH
ON THE HOG.

Now arrange the circled letters
to form the surprise answer, as
suggested by the above cartoon.

Print answer here

JUMBLE®

Unscramble these four Jumbles, one letter
to each square, to form four ordinary words.

GUVEA

HARCO

BROMEY

DACARE

THE THING THAT
EVERY WOMAN HOPES
DOESN'T SHOW.

Now arrange the circled letters
to form the surprise answer, as
suggested by the above cartoon.

Print answer here

Unscramble these four Jumbles, one letter
to each square, to form four ordinary words.

NADDY

YOSIN

SAURES

REBURB

WHAT SHE FELT
HER BOYFRIEND
WAS GIVING HER.

Now arrange the circled letters
to form the surprise answer, as
suggested by the above cartoon.

Print answer here THE ⬡⬡⬡⬡⬡⬡⬡⬡⬡⬡

JUMBLE®

Unscramble these four Jumbles, one letter
to each square, to form four ordinary words.

STRUY

ODITI

DIPTUN

HORBET

WHAT THE
MOTORCYCLE COP
CONSIDERED HIS JOB.

Now arrange the circled letters
to form the surprise answer, as
suggested by the above cartoon.

Print answer here A " ⬡⬡⬡⬡⬡⬡⬡ "

JUMBLE®

Unscramble these four Jumbles, one letter
to each square, to form four ordinary words.

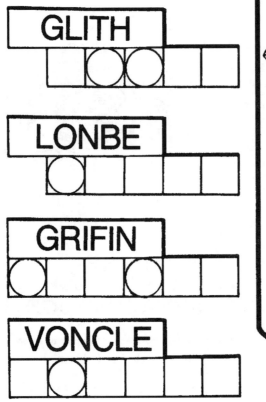

GLITH

LONBE

GRIFIN

VONCLE

SHE GOT BEHIND
IN HER WORK
BECAUSE OF THIS.

Now arrange the circled letters
to form the surprise answer, as
suggested by the above cartoon.

Print answer here HER

JUMBLE®

Unscramble these four Jumbles, one letter
to each square, to form four ordinary words.

TARAP

HOACS

GABNIK

FLANEL

Madame looks
so chic!

THIS BECOMES
A WOMAN.

Now arrange the circled letters
to form the surprise answer, as
suggested by the above cartoon.

Print answer here

JUMBLE®

Unscramble these four Jumbles, one letter to each square, to form four ordinary words.

RUCRY

CAMPH

DEWIST

STABEK

Drivel

WHAT THE LITERARY CAB DRIVER PROVED TO BE.

Now arrange the circled letters to form the surprise answer, as suggested by the above cartoon.

Print answer here

A " ⬡⬡⬡⬡ " ⬡⬡⬡⬡⬡⬡⬡

JUMBLE®

Unscramble these four Jumbles, one letter
to each square, to form four ordinary words.

CUHDY

GANGI

SAYMID

LAMTEL

WHAT THE HAND-
SOME EXERCISE
INSTRUCTOR WAS.

Now arrange the circled letters
to form the surprise answer, as
suggested by the above cartoon.

Print answer here A

Unscramble these four Jumbles, one letter
to each square, to form four ordinary words.

FRACT

PAROE

YARNTT

PINKAD

THE KIND OF
PROBLEMS A SKIPPER
FACES WHEN HIS
SHIP IS BEHIND
SCHEDULE.

Now arrange the circled letters
to form the surprise answer, as
suggested by the above cartoon.

Print answer here

JUMBLE®

Unscramble these four Jumbles, one letter
to each square, to form four ordinary words.

YASOP

DAIBE

INFISH

BARTIB

SOMETHING TO BE
TAKEN WITH A
GRAIN OF SALT.

Now arrange the circled letters
to form the surprise answer, as
suggested by the above cartoon.

Print answer here

Unscramble these four Jumbles, one letter
to each square, to form four ordinary words.

LEREB

KICHT

RACCIT

THROXE

THE OLDEST
REVOLVER IN THE
GUNSMITH'S STUDY.

Now arrange the circled letters
to form the surprise answer, as
suggested by the above cartoon.

Print answer here ⟨◯◯◯⟩ ⟨◯◯◯◯◯⟩

JUMBLE®

Unscramble these four Jumbles, one letter to each square, to form four ordinary words.

HEMRY

DUTIA

HUBLES

POMLEY

Charley says it's a great place

PRIME BEEF

OFTEN LEADS TO A TOUGH STEAK.

Now arrange the circled letters to form the surprise answer, as suggested by the above cartoon.

Print answer here

JUMBLE®

Unscramble these four Jumbles, one letter
to each square, to form four ordinary words.

TUSEG

VELED

VENAHE

FOUNSI

Gosh, boss – you're so shrewd,
so brilliant, so witty...

HOW TO GET A
VAIN MAN EATING
OUT OF YOUR HAND.

Now arrange the circled letters
to form the surprise answer, as
suggested by the above cartoon.

*Print answer
here*

JUMBLE®

Unscramble these four Jumbles, one letter
to each square, to form four ordinary words.

HINKT

GUNST

EXDULP

VARSOY

HOW THE PANTS
ROBBER LEFT THE
BRIDGE PLAYERS.

Now arrange the circled letters
to form the surprise answer, as
suggested by the above cartoon.

*Print
answer
here*

◯◯◯◯◯ - ◯◯◯◯◯◯◯

Unscramble these four Jumbles, one letter
to each square, to form four ordinary words.

HARNC

ACTUD

GOYAVE

MAGITS

THE KIND OF TIME
SHE HAD SHOPPING
FOR A DRESS.

Now arrange the circled letters
to form the surprise answer, as
suggested by the above cartoon.

Print answer here "◯◯◯◯◯◯"

JUMBLE®

Unscramble these four Jumbles, one letter to each square, to form four ordinary words.

THYIC

FOTOA

TOYBAN

MOFTEN

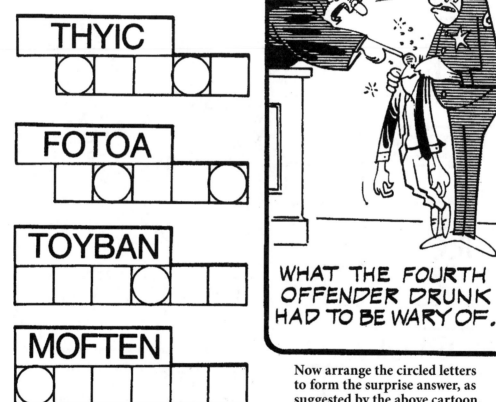

WHAT THE FOURTH OFFENDER DRUNK HAD TO BE WARY OF.

Now arrange the circled letters to form the surprise answer, as suggested by the above cartoon.

Print answer here

JUMBLE®

Unscramble these four Jumbles, one letter
to each square, to form four ordinary words.

FELCT

PLEEX

FULOWE

HORDIA

HOW THE COBBLER
HOPED TO LEAVE
HIS FAMILY.

Now arrange the circled letters
to form the surprise answer, as
suggested by the above cartoon.

Print answer here

⬠⬠⬠⬠ - ⬠⬠⬠⬠⬠⬠

JUMBLE®

Unscramble these four Jumbles, one letter
to each square, to form four ordinary words.

JECET

CLUNE

ORFALL

ACCUST

WHAT THE NEWLY-
MARRIED SALAD
KING BEGGED THE
PRESS TO DO.

Now arrange the circled letters
to form the surprise answer, as
suggested by the above cartoon.

Print
answer
here

" ◯◯◯◯◯◯◯ " ◯◯◯◯◯

JUMBLE®

Unscramble these four Jumbles, one letter
to each square, to form four ordinary words.

HOPAC

MAHRE

RAPTYN

PAWNEO

WHAT LADY GODIVA
SAID AT THE END
OF HER RIDE.

Now arrange the circled letters
to form the surprise answer, as
suggested by the above cartoon.

Print answer here " ⃝⃝⃝⃝ "

JUMBLE®

Unscramble these four Jumbles, one letter
to each square, to form four ordinary words.

LASIA

GINIC

CAGNEY

LAYDED

WHAT THE CHICKEN
FARMER'S PRIZE
ENTRY DID AT THE
COUNTY FAIR.

Now arrange the circled letters
to form the surprise answer, as
suggested by the above cartoon.

Print answer here

JUMBLE®

Unscramble these four Jumbles, one letter
to each square, to form four ordinary words.

TURBS

BEPOR

KORSEM

SAUTLE

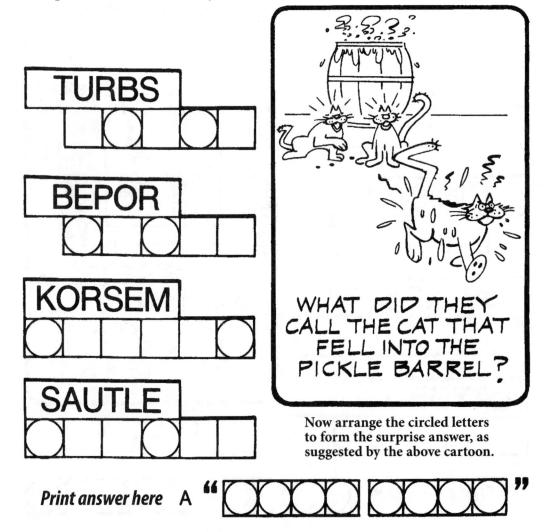

WHAT DID THEY
CALL THE CAT THAT
FELL INTO THE
PICKLE BARREL?

Now arrange the circled letters
to form the surprise answer, as
suggested by the above cartoon.

Print answer here   A " ☐☐☐☐☐ ☐☐☐☐☐ "

JUMBLE®

Unscramble these four Jumbles, one letter to each square, to form four ordinary words.

HUTEC

LOXET

NECCIS

CREBIK

We've all been friends for so long

THE LADIES IN THE SEWING CIRCLE WERE---

Now arrange the circled letters to form the surprise answer, as suggested by the above cartoon.

Print answer here

JUMBLE®

Unscramble these four Jumbles, one letter
to each square, to form four ordinary words.

RIMEN

HAFES

DOHOKE

BOLUDE

Great head for business

SOMETHING LARGELY
RESPONSIBLE FOR
THE PASTA KING'S
SUCCESS.

Now arrange the circled letters
to form the surprise answer, as
suggested by the above cartoon.

Print answer here

JUMBLE®

Unscramble these four Jumbles, one letter
to each square, to form four ordinary words.

ENKLE
◯◯◯◯◯

MEFAL
◯◯◯◯◯

RAWSEN
◯◯◯◯◯◯

TOBUNT
◯◯◯◯◯◯

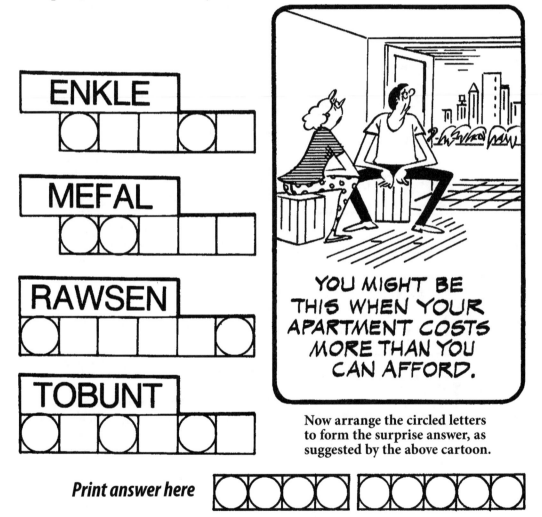

YOU MIGHT BE
THIS WHEN YOUR
APARTMENT COSTS
MORE THAN YOU
CAN AFFORD.

Now arrange the circled letters
to form the surprise answer, as
suggested by the above cartoon.

Print answer here ◯◯◯◯◯ ◯◯◯◯◯

JUMBLE®

Unscramble these four Jumbles, one letter
to each square, to form four ordinary words.

TUXEL

TAGOL

HECARB

FATOLA

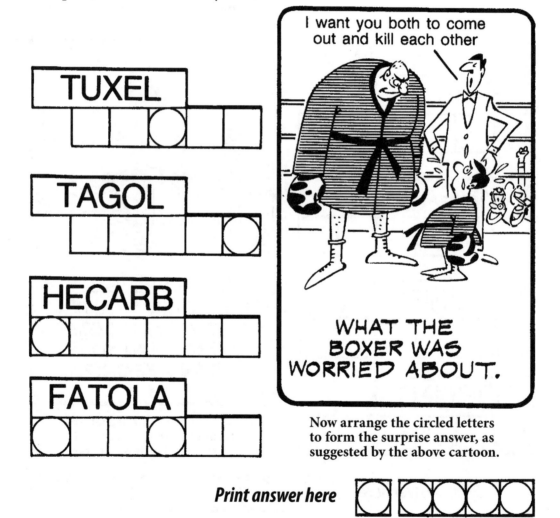

I want you both to come
out and kill each other

WHAT THE
BOXER WAS
WORRIED ABOUT.

Now arrange the circled letters
to form the surprise answer, as
suggested by the above cartoon.

Print answer here

Unscramble these four Jumbles, one letter
to each square, to form four ordinary words.

TIPEY

KEVOE

MAROFT

SOPHIL

WHAT SOME
PEOPLE WHO RUN
FOR OFFICES
PROBABLY DID.

Now arrange the circled letters
to form the surprise answer, as
suggested by the above cartoon.

Print answer here

JUMBLE®

Unscramble these four Jumbles, one letter
to each square, to form four ordinary words.

DRAYT
◯◯□□□

SUDOE
◯□□◯◯

GUBORE
□□◯◯□□

MORTER
◯□□□◯□

WHAT DUNKING
MIGHT BE, BESIDES
BEING BAD
MANNERS.

Now arrange the circled letters
to form the surprise answer, as
suggested by the above cartoon.

Print answer here ◯◯◯◯ ◯◯◯◯◯

JUMBLE®

Unscramble these four Jumbles, one letter
to each square, to form four ordinary words.

YASES

LASIE

GIBNEN

TYGODS

WHERE MANY
FLIERS MAY GET
THEIR BASIC
TRAINING.

Now arrange the circled letters
to form the surprise answer, as
suggested by the above cartoon.

Print answer here ⬚⬚ ⬚⬚⬚⬚⬚

JUMBLE®

Unscramble these four Jumbles, one letter
to each square, to form four ordinary words.

ANUFA

LITTE

TWERPE

SOUNIC

LOOK OUT FOR
THIS WHEN
APPROACHING A
FORK IN THE ROAD.

Now arrange the circled letters
to form the surprise answer, as
suggested by the above cartoon.

Print answer here A ☐☐☐☐☐☐☐☐☐

JUMBLE®

Unscramble these four Jumbles, one letter to each square, to form four ordinary words.

RADIC

ALOCK

SNUFIL

LUTTUM

STOP!!

ONE DOESN'T RUN AFTER THIS.

Now arrange the circled letters to form the surprise answer, as suggested by the above cartoon.

Print answer here THE ◯◯◯◯◯ ◯◯◯◯◯

JUMBLE®

Unscramble these four Jumbles, one letter
to each square, to form four ordinary words.

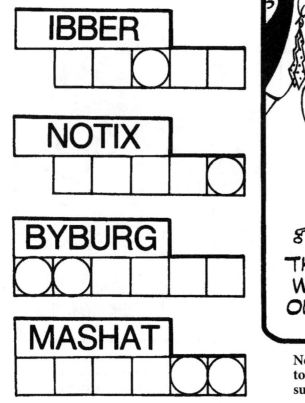

IBBER

NOTIX

BYBURG

MASHAT

Excellent

THIS IS RIGHT
WHEN IT'S LEFT
ON BOTH SIDES.

Now arrange the circled letters
to form the surprise answer, as
suggested by the above cartoon.

Print answer here A

Unscramble these four Jumbles, one letter
to each square, to form four ordinary words.

GEALE

CERDY

NEMDIP

FARIDA

WHAT AN
INEXPERIENCED
RIDER MIGHT GET
WHEN HE FALLS
OFF A HORSE.

Now arrange the circled letters
to form the surprise answer, as
suggested by the above cartoon.

Print answer here ◯◯ - ◯◯◯◯◯

JUMBLE®

Unscramble these four Jumbles, one letter to each square, to form four ordinary words.

ZACER

KLANE

LOYMED

TURBLE

YOU DON'T APPRECIATE THE USEFULNESS OF THIS UNTIL YOU USE IT UP.

Now arrange the circled letters to form the surprise answer, as suggested by the above cartoon.

Print answer here

JUMBLE®

Unscramble these four Jumbles, one letter to each square, to form four ordinary words.

NOLFE

SAUME

YORPTS

BURNEM

One look and I can tell you everything about her

WHAT EXPERIENCED GOSSIPS OFTEN DEPEND ON.

Now arrange the circled letters to form the surprise answer, as suggested by the above cartoon.

Print answer here THEIR ⟨ ⟩⟨ ⟩⟨ ⟩⟨ ⟩⟨ ⟩ ⟨ ⟩⟨ ⟩ ⟨ ⟩⟨ ⟩⟨ ⟩⟨ ⟩⟨ ⟩

JUMBLE®

Unscramble these four Jumbles, one letter
to each square, to form four ordinary words.

KARCC

MYKOS

LORCAR

TEKLET

WHY THE ESCAPED
CON ON THE LAM
TOOK A JOB
ON THE RAILROAD.

Now arrange the circled letters
to form the surprise answer, as
suggested by the above cartoon.

*Print answer
here* TO ◯◯◯◯◯ ◯◯◯◯◯◯◯

JUMBLE®

Unscramble these four Jumbles, one letter to each square, to form four ordinary words.

BECAL

RADAW

FRASIA

CLINPE

WHAT THE ROYAL PARENT WAS TEMPTED TO CALL HIS NEWBORN HEIR.

Now arrange the circled letters to form the surprise answer, as suggested by the above cartoon.

Print answer here ⬡⬡⬡⬡⬡ OF "⬡⬡⬡⬡⬡"

JUMBLE®

Unscramble these four Jumbles, one letter
to each square, to form four ordinary words.

DORRA

BOESE

MERRIP

DOBOLY

The game's
not over!

I'm
quitting!

WHAT A DIETER
WITHOUT WILL
POWER IS.

Now arrange the circled letters
to form the surprise answer, as
suggested by the above cartoon.

Print answer here   A

JUMBLE®

Unscramble these four Jumbles, one letter
to each square, to form four ordinary words.

MICER

FRASC

SHEERA

NAIGAN

HOW THE ENGLISH-
MAN DESCRIBED
HIS WIFE'S DRIVING.

Now arrange the circled letters
to form the surprise answer, as
suggested by the above cartoon.

Print answer here " ◯◯◯◯◯◯◯◯ !"

JUMBLE®

Unscramble these four Jumbles, one letter to each square, to form four ordinary words.

DUIHM

THIRM

REFUGI

YIELDE

WHAT THE NEWLYWED MUSIC LOVERS PLEDGED EACH OTHER.

Now arrange the circled letters to form the surprise answer, as suggested by the above cartoon.

Print answer here

JUMBLE®

Unscramble these four Jumbles, one letter
to each square, to form four ordinary words.

LURBY

CUMIS

FLUITE

NAHDDE

HOW THE
POTTER MAKES
HIS LIVING.

Now arrange the circled letters
to form the surprise answer, as
suggested by the above cartoon.

Print answer here [ ][ ] " [ ][ ][ ][ ] " [ ][ ]

JUMBLE®

Unscramble these four Jumbles, one letter
to each square, to form four ordinary words.

GRABE

KLAYN

HIGLES

TIPECK

WHAT A
PESSIMIST MIGHT
EXPECT TO GET ON
A SILVER PLATTER.

Now arrange the circled letters
to form the surprise answer, as
suggested by the above cartoon.

Print answer here

JUMBLE®

Unscramble these four Jumbles, one letter
to each square, to form four ordinary words.

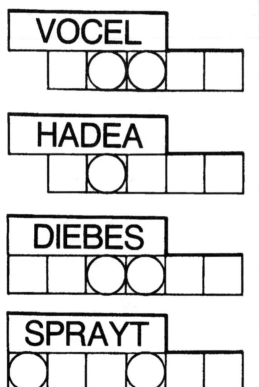

VOCEL

HADEA

DIEBES

SPRAYT

WHAT THE PLAY-
WRIGHT TURNED
GARDENER
WORKED ON.

Now arrange the circled letters
to form the surprise answer, as
suggested by the above cartoon.

Print answer here

JUMBLE®

Unscramble these four Jumbles, one letter
to each square, to form four ordinary words.

TISUE

CREYM

RATVAC

WHOALL

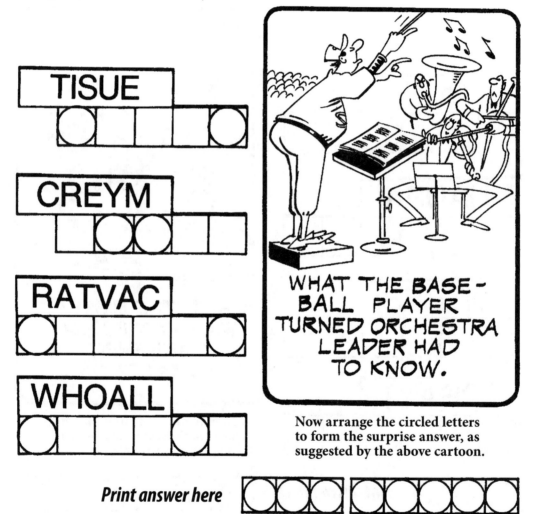

WHAT THE BASE-
BALL PLAYER
TURNED ORCHESTRA
LEADER HAD
TO KNOW.

Now arrange the circled letters
to form the surprise answer, as
suggested by the above cartoon.

Print answer here

JUMBLE®

Unscramble these four Jumbles, one letter to each square, to form four ordinary words.

VALIA

WORBE

MEHRAM

LEWBIA

HOW YOU MIGHT ANNOUNCE THE BIRTH OF A SON TO YOUR FRIENDS.

Now arrange the circled letters to form the surprise answer, as suggested by the above cartoon.

Print answer here BY " ◯◯◯◯ " ◯◯◯◯

Unscramble these four Jumbles, one letter
to each square, to form four ordinary words.

GIMAC
◯◯◯□◯◯

TORNS
◯□◯□◯

CAHBLE
□□◯□◯◯

RESPON
□◯◯◯□□

WHAT SHE SAID WHEN
HE YELLED AT HER
ABOUT THE MONEY
SHE SPENT ON A
CASHMERE COAT.

Now arrange the circled letters
to form the surprise answer, as
suggested by the above cartoon.

Print
answer
here " ◯◯ ' ◯ ◯◯◯◯ ◯◯◯◯ ! "

JUMBLE®

Unscramble these four Jumbles, one letter to each square, to form four ordinary words.

TIMAD

CHITH

GREESY

UNTEAR

WHAT THE HORSE THOUGHT HIS WIFE LOOKED LIKE AS SHE PREPARED FOR BED.

Now arrange the circled letters to form the surprise answer, as suggested by the above cartoon.

Print answer here A ⬡⬡⬡⬡⬡ - ⬡⬡⬡⬡

JUMBLE®

Unscramble these four Jumbles, one letter
to each square, to form four ordinary words.

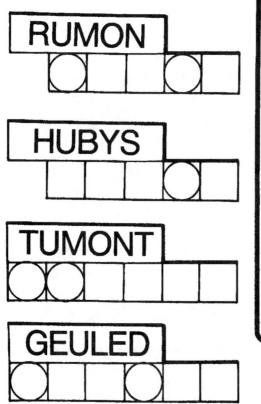

RUMON

HUBYS

TUMONT

GEULED

WHAT THE BORED
PERCUSSION PLAYER
THOUGHT HIS
WORK WAS.

Now arrange the circled letters
to form the surprise answer, as
suggested by the above cartoon.

Print answer here

JUMBLE®

Unscramble these four Jumbles, one letter
to each square, to form four ordinary words.

RAAMO

POSOT

BYSUIL

SEMIED

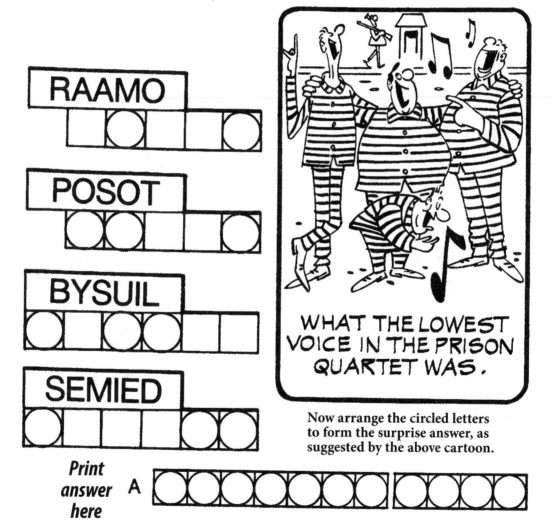

WHAT THE LOWEST
VOICE IN THE PRISON
QUARTET WAS.

Now arrange the circled letters
to form the surprise answer, as
suggested by the above cartoon.

Print
answer
here

A

JUMBLE®

Unscramble these four Jumbles, one letter
to each square, to form four ordinary words.

LYDOM

DATUL

SPOLGE

RICHEP

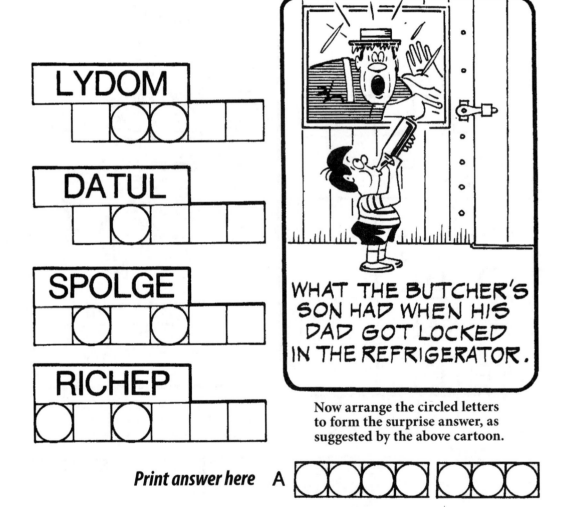

WHAT THE BUTCHER'S
SON HAD WHEN HIS
DAD GOT LOCKED
IN THE REFRIGERATOR.

Now arrange the circled letters
to form the surprise answer, as
suggested by the above cartoon.

Print answer here A ⟨ ⟩⟨ ⟩⟨ ⟩⟨ ⟩ ⟨ ⟩⟨ ⟩⟨ ⟩

JUMBLE®

Unscramble these four Jumbles, one letter
to each square, to form four ordinary words.

LAHCK

SEHCS

DOYLIB

NOPPIL

WHERE WAS THE
FISH WHEN THE
KID PLAYING HOOKY
CAUGHT HIM?

Now arrange the circled letters
to form the surprise answer, as
suggested by the above cartoon.

Print answer here

Unscramble these four Jumbles, one letter
to each square, to form four ordinary words.

UPMEL
◯◯◯ ◯◯

TAIMY
◯◯ ◯◯

CADETH
◯◯◯◯ ◯◯

NAULCY
◯◯◯◯ ◯

WHAT THE WAITER
DID WHEN ASKED
HOW THE SEA-
FOOD WAS.

Now arrange the circled letters
to form the surprise answer, as
suggested by the above cartoon.

Print answer here HE ◯◯◯◯◯◯◯◯ ◯◯

JUMBLE®

Unscramble these four Jumbles, one letter to each square, to form four ordinary words.

ADURF

ESTAE

RUINJY

ROUGAC

WHAT THE ROMANTIC SPANIARD PICKED IN HIS SWEETHEART'S GARDEN.

Now arrange the circled letters to form the surprise answer, as suggested by the above cartoon.

Print answer here

JUMBLE®

Unscramble these four Jumbles, one letter to each square, to form four ordinary words.

PERIT

RAPEP

CAVIDE

ENDECT

BEFORE | AFTER

HOW HAIR THAT WAS PARTED YESTERDAY MAY APPEAR TODAY.

Now arrange the circled letters to form the surprise answer, as suggested by the above cartoon.

Print answer here

JUMBLE®

Unscramble these four Jumbles, one letter to each square, to form four ordinary words.

CORUS

GUJED

HUNCAL

STAPOL

WHAT THE COMICAL SURGEON WAS.

Now arrange the circled letters to form the surprise answer, as suggested by the above cartoon.

Print answer here AN ☐☐☐ ☐☐☐☐☐

JUMBLE®

Unscramble these four Jumbles, one letter
to each square, to form four ordinary words.

THONC

PORDO

DEMIPE

INGUSE

WHAT THE NECKTIE
SALESMEN DID AT
THEIR CONVENTION.

Now arrange the circled letters
to form the surprise answer, as
suggested by the above cartoon.

Print answer here

JUMBLE®

Unscramble these four Jumbles, one letter
to each square, to form four ordinary words.

FLAYE

HOTBO

FACEEF

SAWURL

Sunny
all day

WHAT WEATHER
FORECASTERS
SOMETIMES ARE.

Now arrange the circled letters
to form the surprise answer, as
suggested by the above cartoon.

Print answer here ◯◯◯ ◯◯◯

JUMBLE®

Unscramble these four Jumbles, one letter to each square, to form four ordinary words.

MYLAD
☐ ◯ ◯ ☐ ☐

ZAMIE
☐ ☐ ◯ ◯ ◯

STINCH
◯ ◯ ☐ ◯ ☐ ☐

ENTODE
☐ ◯ ☐ ☐ ◯ ◯

WHAT THE HAY FEVER SUFFERER DID WHEN HE READ ABOUT THE POLLEN COUNT.

Now arrange the circled letters to form the surprise answer, as suggested by the above cartoon.

Print answer here

☐◯◯◯◯◯◯◯ ◯◯ ◯◯

JUMBLE®

Unscramble these four Jumbles, one letter
to each square, to form four ordinary words.

VARNE

THYFE

ALPECA

CAIFLE

WHAT THE
SEASONED COMMUTER
TRIES WHEN HE
FORGETS HIS TICKET.

Now arrange the circled letters
to form the surprise answer, as
suggested by the above cartoon.

Print answer here "◯◯◯◯ ◯◯◯◯"

JUMBLE®

Unscramble these four Jumbles, one letter to each square, to form four ordinary words.

CITOX
◯◯◯◯◯

POUCE
◯◯◯◯◯

TONBEN
◯◯◯◯◯◯

GOAFER
◯◯◯◯◯◯

TELLER

ANOTHER NAME FOR A CHECK FORGER.

Now arrange the circled letters to form the surprise answer, as suggested by the above cartoon.

Print answer here A ◯◯ - ◯◯◯◯◯◯◯

JUMBLE®

Unscramble these four Jumbles, one letter to each square, to form four ordinary words.

LULBY

CARPH

LUFNIX

BASHUM

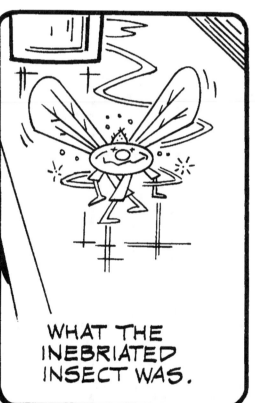

WHAT THE INEBRIATED INSECT WAS.

Now arrange the circled letters to form the surprise answer, as suggested by the above cartoon.

Print answer here A ⬡⬡⬡ ⬡⬡⬡

JUMBLE®

Unscramble these four Jumbles, one letter
to each square, to form four ordinary words.

VEFER

AXORB

TARREY

PEESLY

WHAT THE RED-
CAP WHO WENT
INTO FOREIGN
TRADE WAS.

Now arrange the circled letters
to form the surprise answer, as
suggested by the above cartoon.

Print answer here AN ◯◯ – ◯◯◯◯◯◯

Unscramble these four Jumbles, one letter
to each square, to form four ordinary words.

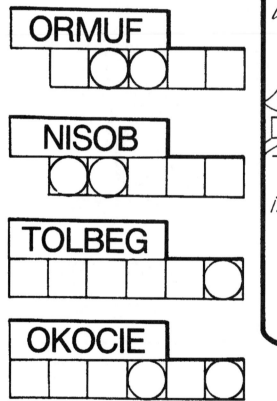

ORMUF

NISOB

TOLBEG

OKOCIE

WHAT HAPPENED
WHEN THE THER-
MOMETER FELL ON
A HOT DAY?

Now arrange the circled letters
to form the surprise answer, as
suggested by the above cartoon.

Print answer here

JUMBLE®

Unscramble these four Jumbles, one letter
to each square, to form four ordinary words.

NAGIT

YOANG

BANACA

CORCUN

WHAT THE FRENCH
CABARET DANCER
KEPT INSISTING.

Now arrange the circled letters
to form the surprise answer, as
suggested by the above cartoon.

**Print answer
here**

JUMBLE

Unscramble these four Jumbles, one letter to each square, to form four ordinary words.

YASSA

GEDUN

THARRE

HARTTO

ALWAYS CHEERED WHEN THEY'RE DOWN AND OUT.

Now arrange the circled letters to form the surprise answer, as suggested by the above cartoon.

Print answer here

JUMBLE®

Unscramble these four Jumbles, one letter
to each square, to form four ordinary words.

DYGUP

NIGGO

SCIBEP

DREVIT

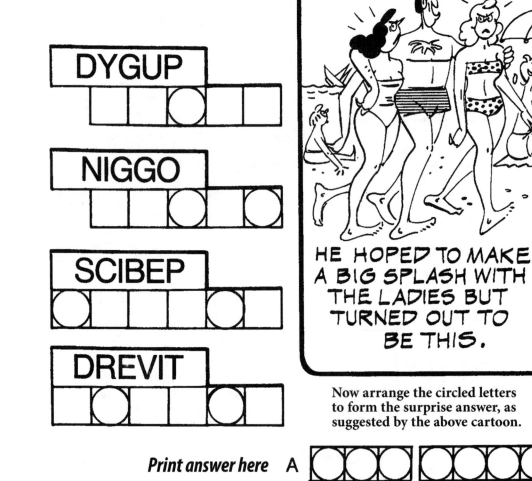

HE HOPED TO MAKE
A BIG SPLASH WITH
THE LADIES BUT
TURNED OUT TO
BE THIS.

Now arrange the circled letters
to form the surprise answer, as
suggested by the above cartoon.

Print answer here A ⬡⬡⬡ ⬡⬡⬡⬡

JUMBLE®

Unscramble these four Jumbles, one letter
to each square, to form four ordinary words.

OUMID

SUHOE

GREFOT

YOUTCH

WHAT THE SHOE
MERCHANT DID
ABOUT HIS BILLS.

Now arrange the circled letters
to form the surprise answer, as
suggested by the above cartoon.

**Print answer
here** HE ☐☐☐☐☐☐ ☐☐☐☐

Unscramble these four Jumbles, one letter
to each square, to form four ordinary words.

JYTET

YORFT

SENTOL

REFOBE

HOW THE TENDER-
FOOT FELT AFTER
HIS FIRST DAY ON
HORSEBACK.

Now arrange the circled letters
to form the surprise answer, as
suggested by the above cartoon.

Print answer here

JUMBLE®

Unscramble these four Jumbles, one letter
to each square, to form four ordinary words.

RANOB

THALC

WEFTES

WAHGIE

WHAT THE
WEREWOLF SAID
WHEN SHE ASKED
FOR MINK.

Now arrange the circled letters
to form the surprise answer, as
suggested by the above cartoon.

Print answer here " ⬚⬚⬚⬚ ⬚⬚⬚⬚ ! "

JUMBLE®

Unscramble these four Jumbles, one letter
to each square, to form four ordinary words.

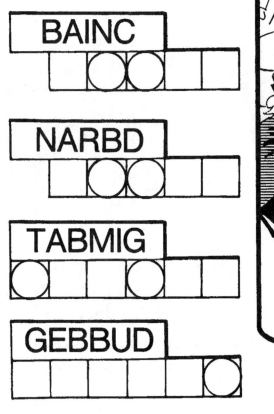

BAINC

NARBD

TABMIG

GEBBUD

WHAT WERE THEY
PLAYING AT THE
PURSE COUNTER?

Now arrange the circled letters
to form the surprise answer, as
suggested by the above cartoon.

Print answer here

JUMBLE®

Unscramble these four Jumbles, one letter
to each square, to form four ordinary words.

TOUHY

HEMIC

TEABED

YENTIC

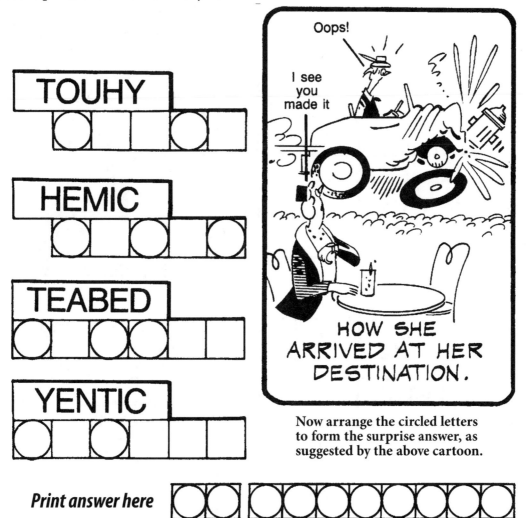

Oops!

I see
you
made it

HOW SHE
ARRIVED AT HER
DESTINATION.

Now arrange the circled letters
to form the surprise answer, as
suggested by the above cartoon.

Print answer here

JUMBLE®

Unscramble these four Jumbles, one letter to each square, to form four ordinary words.

OGOIL

TOARA

HUPNAC

SCUSID

CAR RENTAL AGENCY

THEY CONTRACT TO GIVE YOU A COMFORTABLE RIDE.

Now arrange the circled letters to form the surprise answer, as suggested by the above cartoon.

Print answer here

JUMBLE®

Unscramble these four Jumbles, one letter to each square, to form four ordinary words.

NOMEW

NEEMY

HEBLED

GRAHNE

Ready for surgery

WHAT A DOCTOR
PUTS ON BEFORE
HE STARTS WORKING.

Now arrange the circled letters to form the surprise answer, as suggested by the above cartoon.

Print answer here ☐☐ " ☐ ☐ "

JUMBLE®

Unscramble these four Jumbles, one letter
to each square, to form four ordinary words.

FEBIT

COVAL

RAMPUK

RYTHOF

SILVERWARE

WHAT THEY SAID
WHEN THEY HELD
UP THE SHOP.

Now arrange the circled letters
to form the surprise answer, as
suggested by the above cartoon.

Print answer here

JUMBLE®

Unscramble these four Jumbles, one letter
to each square, to form four ordinary words.

LYKIM

REVUC

SNUFUG

BASURD

THIS CALLS
FOR THE ARMY!

Now arrange the circled letters
to form the surprise answer, as
suggested by the above cartoon.

Print answer here

JUMBLE®

Unscramble these four Jumbles, one letter to each square, to form four ordinary words.

SYNIH

GUCOH

ENCOSH

TAUBEY

WHAT THE TEAM DIDN'T HAVE WHEN IT LOST ITS "SPIRIT."

Now arrange the circled letters to form the surprise answer, as suggested by the above cartoon.

Print answer here

A ☐☐☐☐☐ OF A ☐☐☐☐☐☐

JUMBLE®

Unscramble these four Jumbles, one letter
to each square, to form four ordinary words.

YUINF

SUGIE

DEECES

CRASAF

Busybody!

THOSE WHO TAKE
IT ARE OUT FOR
THE COUNT.

Now arrange the circled letters
to form the surprise answer, as
suggested by the above cartoon.

Print answer here

JUMBLE®

Unscramble these four Jumbles, one letter
to each square, to form four ordinary words.

HIWGE

SCUFO

STEPEL

FLAINE

Vote for me and your government
will take care of you

PEOPLE WOULD
EXPECT THEIR SUP-
PORT FROM CRADLE
TO GRAVE.

Now arrange the circled letters
to form the surprise answer, as
suggested by the above cartoon.

Print answer here

JUMBLE®

Unscramble these four Jumbles, one letter to each square, to form four ordinary words.

LELOH

YARIF

GURDED

BEIMIB

WHAT THE PASSENGERS DID TO THE CONDUCTOR WHEN THE TRAIN WAS LATE.

Now arrange the circled letters to form the surprise answer, as suggested by the above cartoon.

Print answer here " ☐☐☐☐☐☐☐ " AT ☐☐☐

JUMBLE®

Unscramble these four Jumbles, one letter
to each square, to form four ordinary words.

REDEL

STUMY

UNIMME

PHANEP

BANK

TELLER

THEY MAKE
HOLDUPS EASIER.

Now arrange the circled letters
to form the surprise answer, as
suggested by the above cartoon.

Print answer here

JUMBLE®

Unscramble these four Jumbles, one letter to each square, to form four ordinary words.

DICHE

DEUXE

SCUMEL

LARTEY

THE KIND OF
CLOTHES YOU MIGHT
BUY AFTER YOU'VE
LOST WEIGHT.

Now arrange the circled letters to form the surprise answer, as suggested by the above cartoon.

Print answer here " ◯◯◯◯◯◯◯ "

JUMBLE®

Unscramble these four Jumbles, one letter
to each square, to form four ordinary words.

YACKT

YOHEN

CHANIG

LUPPER

Thank goodness my
wife is rich!

PINK
SLIP

THIS COULD SAVE
A HIGH-UP FROM
A PAINFUL
COMEDOWN.

Now arrange the circled letters
to form the surprise answer, as
suggested by the above cartoon.

Print answer here A ⬡⬡⬡⬡⬡⬡⬡⬡⬡⬡⬡

JUMBLE®

Unscramble these four Jumbles, one letter
to each square, to form four ordinary words.

VACHO

NUMIS

BLATUR

TISMEY

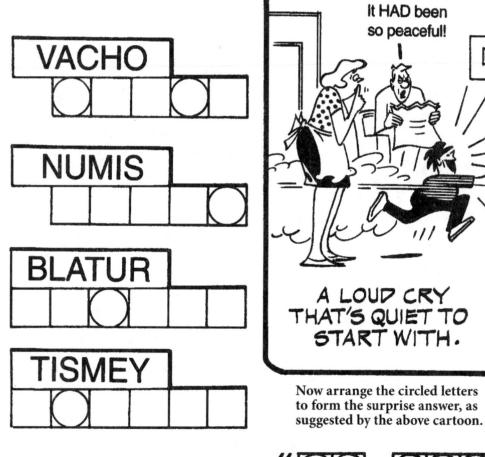

It HAD been
so peaceful!

A LOUD CRY
THAT'S QUIET TO
START WITH.

Now arrange the circled letters
to form the surprise answer, as
suggested by the above cartoon.

Print answer here " ☐☐ - ☐☐☐ "

JUMBLE®

Unscramble these four Jumbles, one letter
to each square, to form four ordinary words.

PLITO

NITLE

FREBLY

GLOANS

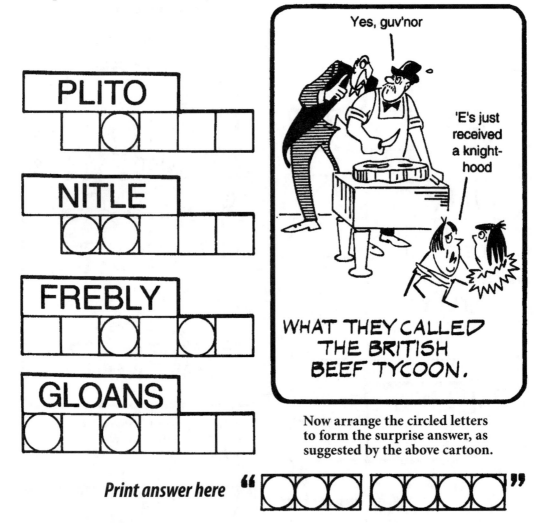

Yes, guv'nor

'E's just
received
a knight-
hood

WHAT THEY CALLED
THE BRITISH
BEEF TYCOON.

Now arrange the circled letters
to form the surprise answer, as
suggested by the above cartoon.

Print answer here " ◯◯◯ ◯◯◯◯ "

JUMBLE®

Unscramble these four Jumbles, one letter to each square, to form four ordinary words.

LUFOR

GOUBS

PREDON

GINRAD

THEY OFTEN GO
OUT TO SEA
IN PORTS.

Now arrange the circled letters
to form the surprise answer, as
suggested by the above cartoon.

Print answer here

JUMBLE®

Unscramble these four Jumbles, one letter to each square, to form four ordinary words.

MARDA

ASTUE

CAFEDE

MUBHEL

Means a lot of hard work

HE SAID THIS WAS THE ACTING GAME.

Now arrange the circled letters to form the surprise answer, as suggested by the above cartoon.

Print answer here

JUMBLE®

Unscramble these four Jumbles, one letter
to each square, to form four ordinary words.

SEECA

SYNAP

INLOOT

LUBOSE

TAKE IN HAND
FOR A BATH!

Now arrange the circled letters
to form the surprise answer, as
suggested by the above cartoon.

Print answer here ⬡⬡⬡⬡

JUMBLE®

Unscramble these four Jumbles, one letter
to each square, to form four ordinary words.

ICMEN

GEDEH

VODURE

TENAGE

— Let's split!

A KIND OF
SURREPTITIOUS
BALL PLAYING.

Now arrange the circled letters
to form the surprise answer, as
suggested by the above cartoon.

Print answer here " ◯◯◯◯◯◯◯◯◯ "

Unscramble these four Jumbles, one letter
to each square, to form four ordinary words.

NUCOE

MYNAL

DOSTIL

SYMICT

Now arrange the circled letters
to form the surprise answer, as
suggested by the above cartoon.

Print answer here ⟨◯◯◯◯◯◯◯◯◯⟩

JUMBLE®

Unscramble these four Jumbles, one letter
to each square, to form four ordinary words.

ROHAB

ISTOC

MYSILF

TANIED

Who's playing the lead?

THE BEST PART
OF THE THEATER.

Now arrange the circled letters
to form the surprise answer, as
suggested by the above cartoon.

Print answer here ☐☐☐ ☐☐☐☐'☐

JUMBLE®

Unscramble these four Jumbles, one letter
to each square, to form four ordinary words.

LANUN

NIORB

TARIPE

TIMOON

MEN IN PORT
ARE CONSPICUOUS.

Now arrange the circled letters
to form the surprise answer, as
suggested by the above cartoon.

Print answer here

JUMBLE®

Unscramble these four Jumbles, one letter
to each square, to form four ordinary words.

MIDIO

PRUNS

REEFIC

HARTOU

THE BACK PART
OF THESE
WEAPONS IS IN
THE CENTER.

Now arrange the circled letters
to form the surprise answer, as
suggested by the above cartoon.

Print answer here " ◯◯ - ◯◯◯◯ - ◯◯ "

JUMBLE®

Unscramble these four Jumbles, one letter to each square, to form four ordinary words.

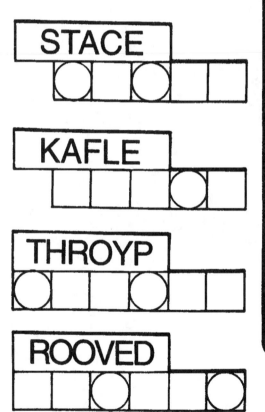

STACE

KAFLE

THROYP

ROOVED

IT'S AGAINST THE LAW TO PICK THEM IN PARKS.

Now arrange the circled letters to form the surprise answer, as suggested by the above cartoon.

Print answer here

161

JUMBLE®

Unscramble these four Jumbles, one letter
to each square, to form four ordinary words.

MEERY

DISTA

SKENIC

TIXECE

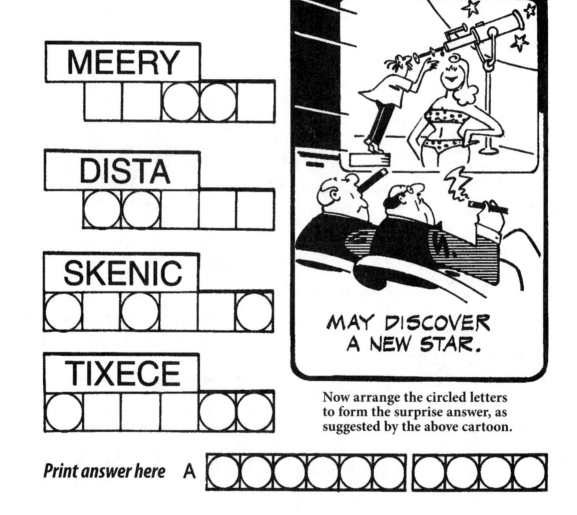

MAY DISCOVER
A NEW STAR.

Now arrange the circled letters
to form the surprise answer, as
suggested by the above cartoon.

Print answer here   A ◯◯◯◯◯◯◯ ◯◯◯◯

JUMBLE®

TIME MACHINE: 1993

Challenger Puzzles

JUMBLE®

Unscramble these six Jumbles, one letter
to each square, to form six ordinary words.

DUGIED

LISHEC

YARPER

JINTEC

DINDAC

SAFTIE

HOW DID THE
ASTRONAUT LIKE
HIS EGGS?

Now arrange the circled letters
to form the surprise answer, as
suggested by the above cartoon.

Print answer here

JUMBLE®

Unscramble these six Jumbles, one letter to each square, to form six ordinary words.

DARNBY

KRODEF

SHRUPE

DANCEN

DOAGIA

ENBATE

Where's Dr. Jekyll?

WHAT GAME WAS HE PLAYING WITH THE POLICE?

Now arrange the circled letters to form the surprise answer, as suggested by the above cartoon.

Print answer here

"◯◯◯◯◯ ◯◯◯ ◯◯◯◯◯"

JUMBLE®

Unscramble these six Jumbles, one letter to each square, to form six ordinary words.

ENGOUL

ENBODY

REPACT

DUBACT

TARRMY

CAFUTE

Great personality!

And such energy!

CHARGE!!!

MAN, THAT FIRE CHIEF SURE WAS THIS!

Now arrange the circled letters to form the surprise answer, as suggested by the above cartoon.

Print answer here

"⬡⬡⬡⬡⬡ - ⬡⬡⬡⬡⬡⬡⬡"

JUMBLE®

Unscramble these six Jumbles, one letter to each square, to form six ordinary words.

YONNAC

REDGUT

CISTEB

TARPET

NOAWHY

NAZATS

WHAT SKUNKS MIGHT PLAY BRIDGE FOR.

Now arrange the circled letters to form the surprise answer, as suggested by the above cartoon.

Print answer here

A

JUMBLE®

Unscramble these six Jumbles, one letter to each square, to form six ordinary words.

IMCUPE

PLOUCE

SHRAID

BOAMEA

BOFRID

ROTHAX

WHAT THE MISSILE EXPERTS WERE MOST CONCERNED WITH.

Now arrange the circled letters to form the surprise answer, as suggested by the above cartoon.

Print answer here

THE ⬡⬡⬡⬡⬡ ⬡⬡⬡ ⬡⬡⬡⬡⬡⬡

JUMBLE®

Unscramble these six Jumbles, one letter to each square, to form six ordinary words.

INGOPE

MOODDE

MELING

NARBEN

TRAFYC

RIMPIA

We're eating too much

I'm afraid to get on a scale

HOW MANY PEOPLE FIND TRAVEL ABROAD.

Now arrange the circled letters to form the surprise answer, as suggested by the above cartoon.

Print answer here

JUMBLE®

Unscramble these six Jumbles, one letter to each square, to form six ordinary words.

YORPET

NOOPUC

DRAMOR

KELCHE

SPOOPE

RELILK

HOW TO GET FISH FOR NOTHING.

Now arrange the circled letters to form the surprise answer, as suggested by the above cartoon.

Print answer here

BY ⬚⬚⬚⬚⬚ ⬚⬚ ⬚⬚⬚⬚⬚⬚

JUMBLE®

Unscramble these six Jumbles, one letter to each square, to form six ordinary words.

ORTRER

SLIMAD

KEWRAH

SISALA

PHONIS

MIDOWS

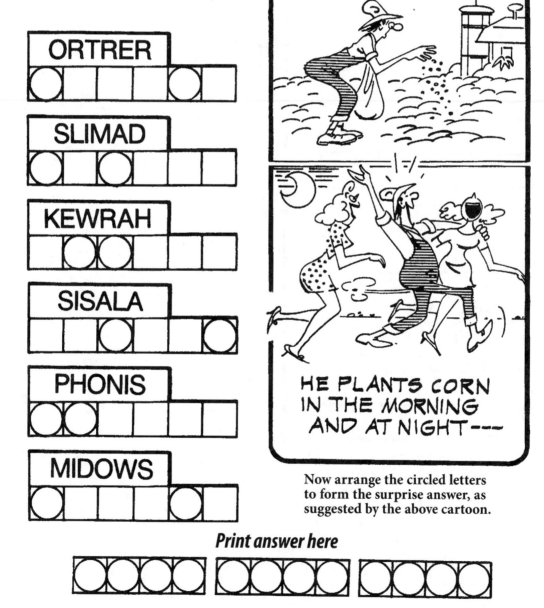

HE PLANTS CORN IN THE MORNING AND AT NIGHT---

Now arrange the circled letters to form the surprise answer, as suggested by the above cartoon.

Print answer here

171

JUMBLE®

Unscramble these six Jumbles, one letter to each square, to form six ordinary words.

MOONID

ALBBUE

CUNESS

LINKUE

INPACT

BELEEF

THE KIND OF STORIES THE GOSSIPY HEN AND COW WERE EXCHANGING.

Now arrange the circled letters to form the surprise answer, as suggested by the above cartoon.

Print answer here

JUMBLE®

Unscramble these six Jumbles, one letter to each square, to form six ordinary words.

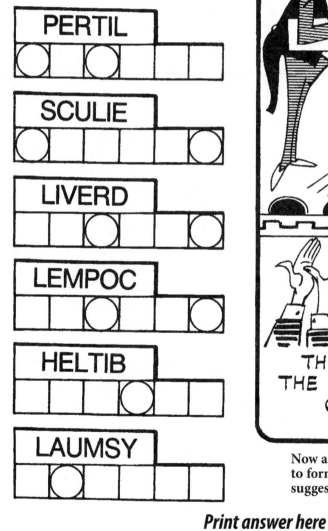

PERTIL

SCULIE

LIVERD

LEMPOC

HELTIB

LAUMSY

THE BIG HIT OF THE SHOW TURNED OUT TO BE---

Now arrange the circled letters to form the surprise answer, as suggested by the above cartoon.

Print answer here

A

JUMBLE®

Unscramble these six Jumbles, one letter to each square, to form six ordinary words.

SHAPIR

INDAGE

TOMSED

RUMMRU

CLOUNK

DEGAMA

M'LADY'S SHOPPE

SOMETHING SHE ALWAYS TOOK ON A SHOPPING TOUR.

Now arrange the circled letters to form the surprise answer, as suggested by the above cartoon.

Print answer here

AN ⬡⬡⬡⬡ TO ⬡⬡⬡⬡⬡⬡⬡

JUMBLE®

Unscramble these six Jumbles, one letter to each square, to form six ordinary words.

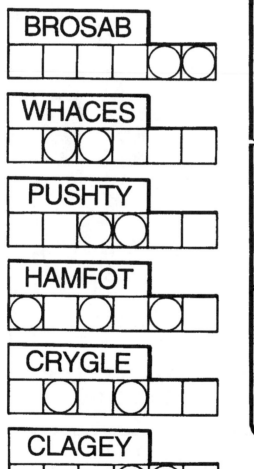

BROSAB

WHACES

PUSHTY

HAMFOT

CRYGLE

CLAGEY

WHAT KEY SHOULD "THE BANANA PEEL SONG" BE SUNG IN?

Now arrange the circled letters to form the surprise answer, as suggested by the above cartoon.

Print answer here

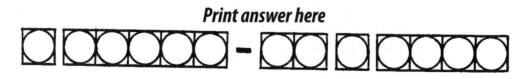

JUMBLE.

Unscramble these six Jumbles, one letter to each square, to form six ordinary words.

VISWEL
⬭⬭☐☐☐☐

LURTIA
⬭☐☐⬭☐☐

TEMNEC
☐☐☐⬭⬭☐

OANNEY
⬭☐☐⬭☐☐

LYMBAC
☐⬭⬭☐☐☐

DAMNET
☐☐☐⬭☐☐

Now behave yourselves!

WHAT STEAMROLLERS MAKE US DO.

Now arrange the circled letters to form the surprise answer, as suggested by the above cartoon.

Print answer here

⬭⬭⬭⬭ ⬭⬭⬭ ⬭⬭⬭⬭

JUMBLE®

Unscramble these six Jumbles, one letter
to each square, to form six ordinary words.

TELBOT

COPITE

TOOSHE

DAYPOR

INPURT

SLABAM

WHAT YOU MIGHT
SEE IN THE
GRANDSTAND.

Now arrange the circled letters
to form the surprise answer, as
suggested by the above cartoon.

Print answer here

A

JUMBLE

Unscramble these six Jumbles, one letter
to each square, to form six ordinary words.

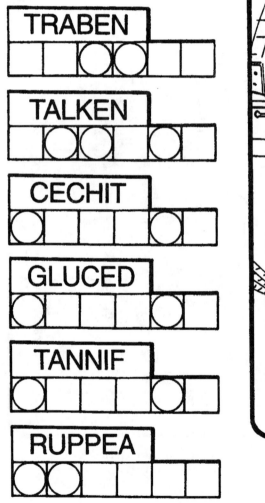

TRABEN

TALKEN

CECHIT

GLUCED

TANNIF

RUPPEA

Not
YOU
again!

WHAT SHE SAID
THE VAMPIRE WAS.

Now arrange the circled letters
to form the surprise answer, as
suggested by the above cartoon.

Print answer here

A

JUMBLE®

Unscramble these six Jumbles, one letter
to each square, to form six ordinary words.

CALARI

WULTOA

LYROOP

RUHNGY

TUGELL

JUINER

Do as I do

WHY THE
PSYCHOLOGIST
TOOK HIS YOUNG
PATIENT BOWLING.

Now arrange the circled letters
to form the surprise answer, as
suggested by the above cartoon.

Print answer here

FOR "◯◯◯◯ – ◯◯◯◯◯◯◯"

JUMBLE®

Unscramble these six Jumbles, one letter to each square, to form six ordinary words.

BUSUDE

ETOGEA

DRAUMA

NUPWOT

THRENE

DYPSOR

WHAT THE MINISTER CALLED THE ICE CREAM PARTY.

Now arrange the circled letters to form the surprise answer, as suggested by the above cartoon.

Print answer here

A ⃝⃝⃝⃝⃝⃝ ⃝⃝⃝⃝⃝⃝

JUMBLE®

Unscramble these six Jumbles, one letter
to each square, to form six ordinary words.

BRANER

HERITH

MUBBEN

CADEED

DROMEN

GROJAN

You're the boss!

WHAT THE TREE
SURGEON BECAME.

Now arrange the circled letters
to form the surprise answer, as
suggested by the above cartoon.

Print answer here

" ⭘⭘⭘⭘⭘⭘ " ⭘⭘⭘⭘⭘⭘⭘

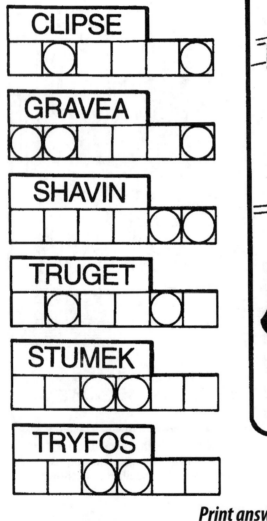

JUMBLE

Unscramble these six Jumbles, one letter to each square, to form six ordinary words.

CLIPSE

GRAVEA

SHAVIN

TRUGET

STUMEK

TRYFOS

WHAT CONGRESS CALLED ITS SOUND SYSTEM.

Now arrange the circled letters to form the surprise answer, as suggested by the above cartoon.

Print answer here

⟨◯◯◯◯◯◯◯◯◯⟩ OF THE ⟨◯◯◯◯◯⟩

182

JUMBLE®

Unscramble these six Jumbles, one letter to each square, to form six ordinary words.

BROWDY

DAGAPO

VELARM

EMBACE

DOLFYN

TASOAN

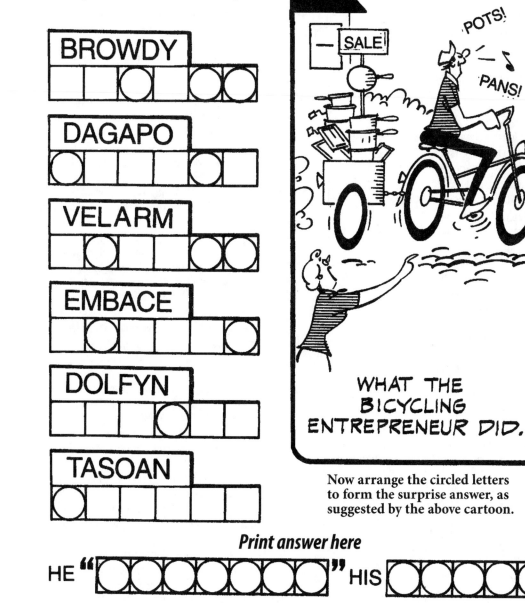

SALE

POTS!

PANS!

WHAT THE BICYCLING ENTREPRENEUR DID.

Now arrange the circled letters to form the surprise answer, as suggested by the above cartoon.

Print answer here

HE "⬡⬡⬡⬡⬡⬡⬡⬡" HIS ⬡⬡⬡⬡⬡

Answers

1. **Jumbles:** MAXIM INKED SATIRE DEVICE
   Answer: What the terrible-tempered sugar grower did—RAISED CANE

2. **Jumbles:** ELEGY TOOTH CAVORT UNSAID
   Answer: A person who makes little things count—A TEACHER

3. **Jumbles:** STEED IRATE GUNNER MARROW
   Answer: What jaywalkers may be wearing tomorrow—WINGS

4. **Jumbles:** PAGAN DOWDY BEDECK FURROW
   Answer: What a few catty remarks turned the ladies' lounge into—A POWDER KEG

5. **Jumbles:** CAPON RAPID NUDISM TIMELY
   Answer: What the egotist was suffering from—"I" STRAIN

6. **Jumbles:** SHAKY HOARD MOTIVE JESTER
   Answer: What the cute little potato was warned against—MASHERS

7. **Jumbles:** IRONY JOUST NOTIFY CURFEW
   Answer: What the chiropractor and his wife were working on—A JOINT RETURN

8. **Jumbles:** MOSSY GROUP MORGUE EITHER
   Answer: What boarding house gossip used to start with—"ROOMERS"

9. **Jumbles:** BASSO ARMOR TACKLE STUCCO
   Answer: What the twelve bottles of moonshine eventually became—A COURT CASE

10. **Jumbles:** TASTY PRIME ENOUGH ABUSED
    Answer: What you might get from a SENATOR—"NO TEARS"

11. **Jumbles:** FUDGE VISTA UNCLAD ENTICE
    Answer: Rather big for ballet these days—AUDIENCES

12. **Jumbles:** MOUNT FILMY INFIRM GALAXY
    Answer: What horsemeat is to a dog—"FILLY" MIGNON

13. **Jumbles:** LIBEL BLAZE UNEASY ADMIRE
    Answer: What she was after posing for a full-length portrait—ALL IN

14. **Jumbles:** MEALY GUESS PURIFY ENTAIL
    Answer: We close our eyes to this—SLEEP

15. **Jumbles:** BLIMP HOBBY NIMBLE DRAGON
    Answer: Where the overzealous cow gave her milk—BEYOND THE "PAIL"

16. **Jumbles:** ERASE TULIP TORRID QUIVER
    Answer: What the prison designer created—QUITE A STIR

17. **Jumbles:** HABIT MADAM GUITAR FORMAL
    Answer: Someone who raids the refrigerator for a midnight snack—A "HAM-BURGLAR"

18. **Jumbles:** LINGO UNWED HERMIT CRAYON
    Answer: It's usual to have this before dinner—LUNCH

19. **Jumbles:** WAGON BUMPY LATEST NEARLY
    Answer: What his old flame did when she saw him with another girl—A SLOW BURN

20. **Jumbles:** WHEEL EMBER BIKINI LARYNX
    Answer: What the traveling correspondent's wife didn't like—HIS "BYE LINE"

21. **Jumbles:** DRAFT EMPTY INVERT REFUGE
    Answer: You can always grow this in your garden if you work hard enough—TIRED

22. **Jumbles:** SWAMP TEMPO HEALTH PREFER
    Answer: What the restaurant on the moon lacked—ATMOSPHERE

23. **Jumbles:** IMBUE CHOKE TANGLE DOUBLY
    Answer: Something besides the tide which the moon affects—THE UNTIED

24. **Jumbles:** COWER JULEP TRIBAL ANEMIA
    Answer: What you might call this barber's establishment—A CLIP JOINT

25. **Jumbles:** HANDY GAUDY DEAFEN RADIUS
    Answer: What did the exuberant wife do when her husband struck oil?—SHE GUSHED

26. **Jumbles:** RODEO FAVOR THIRTY BRIDLE
    Answer: What she called her sourpuss husband—HER BITTER HALF

27. **Jumbles:** PROVE FETID NIBBLE ORIGIN
    Answer: The boxer's smooth line finally got him this—ROPED IN

28. **Jumbles:** CARGO KNIFE PEPTIC KITTEN
    Answer: A man whose work requires him to grasp things quickly—A PICKPOCKET

29. **Jumbles:** GROOM FOAMY NUANCE SINGLE
    Answer: What her earnings often don't keep up with—HER YEARNINGS

30. **Jumbles:** ALIVE OFTEN DREDGE CAMPUS
    Answer: What the sailor became when he married a widow—A SECOND MATE

31. **Jumbles:** VIGIL TRILL TRICKY NEPHEW
    Answer: Those stories told by the construction worker were—RIVETING

32. **Jumbles:** YODEL EXACT OPAQUE PYTHON
    Answer: What do you call an officer who lost the key to his house?—A "COP OUT"

33. **Jumbles:** UPPER TROTH BIGAMY IMPUGN
    Answer: What he did when he ran into his pal—PUT THE BITE ON HIM

34. **Jumbles:** HAVEN TEPID GENDER UNHOLY
    Answer: Penthouse dwellers usually pay this—HIGH RENT

35. **Jumbles:** EVENT FLOOR FITFUL TANKER
    Answer: One of the identical twins was five feet tall—what was the other?—FIVE FEET, TOO

36. **Jumbles:** MAUVE TRULY SCHEME REDEEM
    Answer: People in love seldom travel in these—THREES

37. **Jumbles:** SUEDE LILAC ADROIT RARITY
    Answer: What some people travel in while remaining at home—TRAILERS

38. **Jumbles:** PLUSH FRAME OFFSET FLAUNT
    Answer: These are stuck outside and also could be stuck unstuck inside—STAMPS

39. **Jumbles:** BYLAW PIOUS GRIMLY SCORCH
    Answer: What a crime wave gets in the newspaper—A BIG SPLASH

40. **Jumbles:** ENTRY CATCH MISFIT EXHALE
    Answer: High heels can often be this—"ARCH" ENEMIES

41. **Jumbles:** FLANK SWOOP FEUDAL PODIUM
    Answer: In the theater, these mean no work and no play—FLOPS

42. **Jumbles:** TAWNY PIECE BOUNTY TOWARD
    Answer: What the umpire turned pizza chef announced—"BATTER UP!"

43. **Jumbles:** DEITY VITAL RAREFY EXTENT
    Answer: His business success depends on driving customers away—A TAXI DRIVER

44. **Jumbles:** VOUCH GLADE TARGET AROUSE
Answer: What the lumberjack went downstream on—
A "TRAVELOG"

45. **Jumbles:** TWILL METAL FIASCO HANDLE
Answer: What a deep-sea diver must do when he has a
problem—FATHOM IT

46. **Jumbles:** FEWER LYING HUNTER ABOUND
Answer: What do you call a humorist with a split
personality?—A HALF WIT

47. **Jumbles:** PENCE UTTER FABLED EFFIGY
Answer: What the new owner of the run-down steak house tried
to do—BEEF IT UP

48. **Jumbles:** QUAIL LOGIC CANKER LOCATE
Answer: What the camera club members called themselves—
A CLICK CLIQUE

49. **Jumbles:** INEPT LEECH DIGEST CLAUSE
Answer: The flaw in the butcher's golf game—HIS SLICE

50. **Jumbles:** MOUND CHEEK EMBODY BEHAVE
Answer: How the lazy gardener felt about his work—HOE HUM

51. **Jumbles:** OUTDO PATIO INVENT FINERY
Answer: What the commercial fisherman lived on—NET PROFIT

52. **Jumbles:** GRAIN CHAFE OMELET COERCE
Answer: What the melancholy painter made—A LONG FACE

53. **Jumbles:** DOILY BLESS UNIQUE HAZING
Answer: What the matador turned road builder liked most
about his work—THE BULLDOZING

54. **Jumbles:** LEAKY PLAIT AGENDA BEHIND
Answer: This can turn a shoe into a slipper—A BANANA PEEL

55. **Jumbles:** MESSY DOWDY TIDBIT SUNDAE
Answer: What the epidemic of measles in Geneva created—
DOTTED SWISS

56. **Jumbles:** CLOUT ALBUM FACADE HOMAGE
Answer: What it takes to get these two all fired up—A MATCH

57. **Jumbles:** BASIN KNOWN CORPSE FACING
Answer: What he was as a result of teaching his teenager to
drive—A WRECK

58. **Jumbles:** TRYST TIGER NEARBY TINGLE
Answer: What she served the handsome depositor with—
INTEREST

59. **Jumbles:** NAVAL TABOO COHORT DAWNED
Answer: What the snowball fight proved to be—A COLD WAR

60. **Jumbles:** NOOSE NIECE TARTAR FERVOR
Answer: The part of the book the podiatrist liked best—
THE FOOTNOTES

61. **Jumbles:** TOKEN BELLE ADRIFT FLORID
Answer: The kind of gift some youngsters might kick about—
A FOOTBALL

62. **Jumbles:** SLANT MINOR FACIAL REBUKE
Answer: What the math genius with small kids knew all about—
FORMULAS

63. **Jumbles:** GRIEF PROXY AERATE CAMPER
Answer: What the two tycoons discussed at a luncheon
conference—A MERGER

64. **Jumbles:** DRONE HAIRY FOSSIL TRAGIC
Answer: How a championship runner might take a high
hurdle—IN HIS STRIDE

65. **Jumbles:** GAILY BASIC ABLAZE ICEBOX
Answer: What the computer repairman's nickname was—
"BIG BILL"

66. **Jumbles:** NEWLY WINCE ALWAYS FICKLE
Answer: A low-down joint—AN ANKLE

67. **Jumbles:** BEGUN FLUKE TYPING ORPHAN
Answer: The first thing you plant in your garden—YOUR FEET

68. **Jumbles:** FUNNY EIGHT ENTITY PLACID
Answer: Where you may wind up if you live too high on the
hog—IN THE PEN

69. **Jumbles:** VAGUE ROACH EMBRYO ARCADE
Answer: The thing that every woman hopes doesn't show—
HER AGE

70. **Jumbles:** DANDY NOISY ASSURE RUBBER
Answer: What she felt her boyfriend was giving her—
THE RUNAROUND

71. **Jumbles:** RUSTY IDIOT PUNDIT BOTHER
Answer: What the motorcycle cop considered his job—
A "PURSUIT"

72. **Jumbles:** LIGHT NOBLE FIRING CLOVEN
Answer: She got behind in her work because of this—
HER FILING

73. **Jumbles:** APART CHAOS BAKING FALLEN
Answer: This becomes a woman—A GIRL

74. **Jumbles:** CURRY CHAMP WIDEST BASKET
Answer: What the literary cab driver proved to be—
A "HACK" WRITER

75. **Jumbles:** DUCHY AGING DISMAY MALLET
Answer: What the handsome exercise instructor was—
A GYM DANDY

76. **Jumbles:** CRAFT OPERA TYRANT KIDNAP
Answer: The kind of problems a skipper faces when his ship is
behind schedule—KNOTTY

77. **Jumbles:** SOAPY ABIDE FINISH RABBIT
Answer: Something to be taken with a grain of salt—A RADISH

78. **Jumbles:** REBEL THICK ARCTIC EXHORT
Answer: The oldest revolver in the gunsmith's study—
THE EARTH

79. **Jumbles:** RHYME AUDIT BUSHEL EMPLOY
Answer: Often leads to a tough steak—A BUM STEER

80. **Jumbles:** GUEST DELVE HEAVEN FUSION
Answer: How to get a vain man eating out of your hand—
FEED HIS EGO

81. **Jumbles:** THINK STUNG DUPLEX SAVORY
Answer: How the pants robber left the bridge players—
SHORT-SUITED

82. **Jumbles:** RANCH DUCAT VOYAGE STIGMA
Answer: The kind of time she had shopping for a dress—
"TRYING"

83. **Jumbles:** ITCHY AFOOT BOTANY FOMENT
Answer: What the fourth offender drunk had to be wary of—
A FIFTH

84. **Jumbles:** CLEFT EXPEL WOEFUL HAIRDO
Answer: How the cobbler hoped to leave his family—
WELL-HEELED

85. **Jumbles:** EJECT UNCLE FLORAL CACTUS
Answer: What the newly married salad king begged the press to
do—"LETTUCE" ALONE

86. **Jumbles:** POACH HAREM PANTRY WEAPON
Answer: What Lady Godiva said at the end of her ride—
"WHOA"

87. **Jumbles:** ALIAS ICING AGENCY DEADLY
Answer: What the chicken farmer's prize entry did at the county
fair—LAID AN EGG

88. **Jumbles:** BURST PROBE SMOKER SALUTE
Answer: What did they call the cat that fell into the pickle
barrel?—A "SOUR PUSS"

89. **Jumbles:** CHUTE EXTOL SCENIC BICKER
Answer: The ladies in the sewing circle were—CLOSE KNIT

90. **Jumbles:** MINER SHEAF HOOKED DOUBLE
Answer: Something largely responsible for the pasta king's success—HIS NOODLE

91. **Jumbles:** KNEEL FLAME ANSWER BUTTON
Answer: You might be this when your apartment costs more than you can afford—FLAT BROKE

92. **Jumbles:** EXULT GLOAT BREACH AFLOAT
Answer: What the boxer was worried about—A BOUT

93. **Jumbles:** PIETY EVOKE FORMAT POLISH
Answer: What some people who run for offices probably did—OVERSLEPT

94. **Jumbles:** TARDY DOUSE BROGUE TREMOR
Answer: What dunking might be, besides being bad manners—GOOD TASTE

95. **Jumbles:** ESSAY AISLE BENIGN STODGY
Answer: Where many fliers may get their basic training—IN NESTS

96. **Jumbles:** FAUNA TITLE PEWTER COUSIN
Answer: Look out for this when approaching a fork in the road—A PUNCTURE

97. **Jumbles:** ACRID CLOAK SINFUL TUMULT
Answer: One doesn't run after this—THE LAST TRAIN

98. **Jumbles:** BRIBE TOXIN GRUBBY ASTHMA
Answer: This is right when it's left on both sides—A MARGIN

99. **Jumbles:** EAGLE DECRY IMPEND AFRAID
Answer: What an inexperienced rider might get when he falls off a horse—DE-RIDED

100. **Jumbles:** CRAZE ANKLE MELODY BUTLER
Answer: You don't appreciate the usefulness of this until you use it up—AN UMBRELLA

101. **Jumbles:** FELON AMUSE SPORTY NUMBER
Answer: What experienced gossips often depend on—THEIR SENSE OF RUMOR

102. **Jumbles:** CRACK SMOKY CORRAL KETTLE
Answer: Why the escaped con on the lam took a job on the railroad—TO MAKE TRACKS

103. **Jumbles:** CABLE AWARD SAFARI PENCIL
Answer: What the royal parent was tempted to call his newborn heir—PRINCE OF "WAILS"

104. **Jumbles:** ARDOR OBESE PRIMER BLOODY
Answer: What a dieter without will power is—A POOR LOSER

105. **Jumbles:** CRIME SCARF HEARSE ANGINA
Answer: How the Englishman described his wife's driving—"SMASHING!"

106. **Jumbles:** HUMID MIRTH FIGURE EYELID
Answer: What the newlywed music lovers pledged to each other—HIGH FIDELITY

107. **Jumbles:** BURLY MUSIC FUTILE HANDED
Answer: How the potter makes his living—HE "URNS" IT

108. **Jumbles:** BARGE LANKY SLEIGH PICKET
Answer: What a pessimist might expect to get on a silver platter—TARNISH

109. **Jumbles:** CLOVE AHEAD BESIDE PASTRY
Answer: What the playwright turned gardener worked on—HIS PLOT

110. **Jumbles:** SUITE MERCY CRAVAT HALLOW
Answer: What the baseball player turned orchestra leader had to know—THE SCORE

111. **Jumbles:** AVAIL BOWER HAMMER BEWAIL
Answer: How you might announce the birth of a son to your friends—BY "HEIR" MAIL

112. **Jumbles:** MAGIC SNORT BLEACH PERSON
Answer: What she said when he yelled at her about the money she spent on a cashmere coat—"IT'S MERE CASH!"

113. **Jumbles:** ADMIT HITCH GEYSER NATURE
Answer: What the horse thought his wife looked like as she prepared for bed—A NIGHT-MARE

114. **Jumbles:** MOURN BUSHY MUTTON DELUGE
Answer: What the bored percussion player thought his work was—HUMDRUM

115. **Jumbles:** AROMA STOOP BUSILY DEMISE
Answer: What the lowest voice in the prison quartet was—A STRIPED BASS

116. **Jumbles:** MOLDY ADULT GOSPEL CIPHER
Answer: What the butcher's son had when his dad got locked in the refrigerator—A COLD POP

117. **Jumbles:** CHALK CHESS BODILY POPLIN
Answer: Where was the fish when the kid playing hooky caught him?—IN A SCHOOL

118. **Jumbles:** PLUME AMITY DETACH LUNACY
Answer: What the waiter did when asked how the seafood was—HE CLAMMED UP

119. **Jumbles:** FRAUD TEASE INJURY COUGAR
Answer: What the romantic Spaniard picked in his sweetheart's garden—A GUITAR

120. **Jumbles:** TRIPE PAPER ADVICE DECENT
Answer: How hair that was parted yesterday may appear today—DEPARTED

121. **Jumbles:** SCOUR JUDGE LAUNCH POSTAL
Answer: What the comical surgeon was—AN OLD CUTUP

122. **Jumbles:** NOTCH DROOP IMPEDE GENIUS
Answer: What the necktie salesmen did at their convention—TIED ONE ON

123. **Jumbles:** LEAFY BOOTH EFFACE WALRUS
Answer: What weather forecasters sometimes are—ALL WET

124. **Jumbles:** MADLY MAIZE SNITCH DENOTE
Answer: What the hay fever sufferer did when he read about the pollen count—SNEEZED AT IT

125. **Jumbles:** RAVEN HEFTY PALACE FACILE
Answer: What the seasoned commuter tries when he forgets his ticket—"FARE PLAY"

126. **Jumbles:** TOXIC COUPE BONNET FORAGE
Answer: Another name for a check forger—A NO-ACCOUNT

127. **Jumbles:** BULLY PARCH INFLUX AMBUSH
Answer: What the inebriated insect was—A BAR FLY

128. **Jumbles:** FEVER BORAX ARTERY SLEEPY
Answer: What the redcap who went into foreign trade was—AN EX-PORTER

129. **Jumbles:** FORUM BISON GOBLET COOKIE
Answer: What happened when the thermometer fell on a hot day?—IT BROKE

130. **Jumbles:** GIANT AGONY CABANA CONCUR
Answer: What the French cabaret dancer kept insisting—I CAN CANCAN

131. **Jumbles:** ASSAY NUDGE RATHER THROAT
Answer: Always cheered when they're down and out—ASTRONAUTS

132. **Jumbles:** PUDGY GOING BICEPS DIVERT
Answer: He hoped to make a big splash with the ladies but turned out to be this—A BIG DRIP

133. **Jumbles:** ODIUM HOUSE FORGET TOUCHY
Answer: What the shoe merchant did about his bills—
HE FOOTED THEM

134. **Jumbles:** JETTY FORTY STOLEN BEFORE
Answer: How the tenderfoot felt after his first day on
horseback—BETTER OFF

135. **Jumbles:** BARON LATCH FEWEST AWEIGH
Answer: What the werewolf said when she asked for mink—
"WEAR WOLF!"

136. **Jumbles:** CABIN BRAND GAMBIT BEDBUG
Answer: What were they playing at the purse counter?—
GRAB BAG

137. **Jumbles:** YOUTH CHIME DEBATE NICETY
Answer: How she arrived at her destination—BY ACCIDENT

138. **Jumbles:** IGLOO AORTA PAUNCH DISCUS
Answer: They contract to give you a comfortable ride—SPRINGS

139. **Jumbles:** WOMEN ENEMY BEHELD HANGER
Answer: What a doctor puts on before he starts working—
AN "M D"

140. **Jumbles:** BEFIT VOCAL MARKUP FROTHY
Answer: What they said when they held up the shop—
FORK IT OVER

141. **Jumbles:** MILKY CURVE FUNGUS ABSURD
Answer: This calls for the army!—A BUGLE

142. **Jumbles:** SHINY COUGH CHOSEN BEAUTY
Answer: What the team didn't have when it lost its "spirit"—
A GHOST OF A CHANCE

143. **Jumbles:** UNIFY GUISE SECEDE FRACAS
Answer: Those who take it are out for the count—CENSUS

144. **Jumbles:** WEIGH FOCUS PESTLE FINALE
Answer: People would expect their support from cradle to
grave—LEGS

145. **Jumbles:** HELLO FAIRY DRUDGE IMBIBE
Answer: What the passengers did to the conductor when the
train was late—"RAILED" AT HIM

146. **Jumbles:** ELDER MUSTY IMMUNE HAPPEN
Answer: They make holdups easier—HANDLES

147. **Jumbles:** CHIDE EXUDE MUSCLE REALTY
Answer: The kind of clothes you might buy after you've lost
weight—"REDUCED"

148. **Jumbles:** TACKY HONEY ACHING PURPLE
Answer: This could save a high-up from a painful comedown—
A PARACHUTE

149. **Jumbles:** HAVOC MINUS BRUTAL STYMIE
Answer: A loud cry that's quiet to start with—"SH-OUT"

150. **Jumbles:** PILOT INLET BELFRY SLOGAN
Answer: What they called the British beef tycoon—"SIR LOIN"

151. **Jumbles:** FLOUR BOGUS PONDER DARING
Answer: They often go out to sea in ports—PIERS

152. **Jumbles:** DRAMA SAUTE DEFACE HUMBLE
Answer: He said this was the acting game—CHARADES

153. **Jumbles:** CEASE PANSY LOTION BLOUSE
Answer: Take in hand for a bath!—SOAP

154. **Jumbles:** MINCE HEDGE DEVOUR NEGATE
Answer: A kind of surreptitious ball playing—"UNDERHAND"

155. **Jumbles:** OUNCE MANLY STOLID MYSTIC
Answer: In a word, it means the same thing!—SYNONYM

156. **Jumbles:** ABHOR STOIC FLIMSY DETAIN
Answer: The best part of the theater—THE STAR'S

157. **Jumbles:** ANNUL ROBIN PIRATE MOTION
Answer: MEN IN PORT are conspicuous—PROMINENT

158. **Jumbles:** IDIOM SPURN FIERCE AUTHOR
Answer: The back part of these weapons is in the center—
"FI-REAR-MS"

159. **Jumbles:** CASTE FLAKE TROPHY OVERDO
Answer: It's against the law to pick them in parks—POCKETS

160. **Jumbles:** EMERY STAID SICKEN EXCITE
Answer: May discover a new star—A SCREEN TEST

161. **Jumbles:** GUIDED CHISEL PRAYER INJECT CANDID FIESTA
Answer: How did the astronaut like his eggs?—STRAIGHT UP

162. **Jumbles:** BRANDY FORKED PUSHER CANNED ADAGIO BEATEN
Answer: What game was he playing with the police?—
"HYDE AND SEEK"

163. **Jumbles:** LOUNGE BEYOND CARPET ABDUCT MARTYR FAUCET
Answer: Man, that fire chief sure was this!—"FLAME-BUOYANT"

164. **Jumbles:** CANYON TRUDGE BISECT PATTER ANYHOW STANZA
Answer: What skunks might play bridge for—A SCENT A POINT

165. **Jumbles:** PUMICE COUPLE RADISH AMOEBA FORBID THORAX
Answer: What the missile experts were most concerned with—
THE RACE FOR SPACE

166. **Jumbles:** PIGEON DOOMED MINGLE BANNER CRAFTY IMPAIR
Answer: How many people find travel abroad—BROADENING

167. **Jumbles:** POETRY COUPON RAMROD HECKLE OPPOSE KILLER
Answer: How to get fish for nothing—BY HOOK OR CROOK

168. **Jumbles:** TERROR DISMAL HAWKER ASSAIL SIPHON WISDOM
Answer: He plants corn in the morning and at night—
SOWS WILD OATS

169. **Jumbles:** DOMINO BAUBLE CENSUS UNLIKE CATNIP FEEBLE
Answer: The kind of stories the gossipy hen and cow were
exchanging—COCK AND BULL

170. **Jumbles:** TRIPLE SLUICE DRIVEL COMPEL BLITHE ASYLUM
Answer: The big hit of the show turned out to be—
A LITTLE MISS

171. **Jumbles:** PARISH GAINED MODEST MURMUR UNLOCK DAMAGE
Answer: Something she always took on a shopping tour—
AN URGE TO SPLURGE

172. **Jumbles:** ABSORB CASHEW TYPHUS FATHOM CLERGY LEGACY
Answer: What key should "The Banana Peel Song" be sung
in?—C SHARP—OR B FLAT

173. **Jumbles:** SWIVEL RITUAL CEMENT ANYONE CYMBAL TANDEM
Answer: What steamrollers make us do—MEND OUR WAYS

174. **Jumbles:** BOTTLE POETIC SOOTHE PARODY TURNIP BALSAM
Answer: What you might see in the grandstand—
A SPECTATOR SPORT

175. **Jumbles:** BANTER ANKLET HECTIC CUDGEL INFANT PAUPER
Answer: What she said the vampire was—A PAIN IN THE NECK

176. **Jumbles:** RACIAL POORLY GULLET OUTLAW HUNGRY INJURE
Answer: Why the psychologist took his young patient
bowling—FOR "ROLL-PLAYING"

177. **Jumbles:** SUBDUE MARAUD NETHER GOATEE UPTOWN DROPSY
Answer: What the minister called the ice cream party—
A SUNDAE SERMON

178. **Jumbles:** BARREN BENUMB MODERN HITHER DECADE JARGON
Answer: What the tree surgeon became—"BRANCH" MANAGER

179. **Jumbles:** SPLICE VANISH MUSKET RAVAGE GUTTER FROSTY
Answer: What Congress called its sound system—
SPEAKERS OF THE HOUSE

180. **Jumbles:** BYWORD MARVEL FONDLY PAGODA BECAME SONATA
Answer: What the bicycling entrepreneur did—
HE "PEDDLED" HIS WARES

Need More Jumbles?

Jumble® Books

More than 175 puzzles each!

Cowboy Jumble®
$10.95 • ISBN: 978-1-62937-355-3

Jammin' Jumble®
$9.95 • ISBN: 978-1-57243-844-6

Java Jumble®
$10.95 • ISBN: 978-1-60078-415-6

Jet Set Jumble®
$9.95 • ISBN: 978-1-60078-353-1

Jolly Jumble®
$10.95 • ISBN: 978-1-60078-214-5

Jumble® Anniversary
$10.95 • ISBN: 987-1-62937-734-6

Jumble® Ballet
$10.95 • ISBN: 978-1-62937-616-5

Jumble® Birthday
$10.95 • ISBN: 978-1-62937-652-3

Jumble® Celebration
$10.95 • ISBN: 978-1-60078-134-6

Jumble® Champion
$10.95 • ISBN: 978-1-62937-870-1

Jumble® Coronation
$10.95 • ISBN: 978-1-62937-976-0

Jumble® Cuisine
$10.95 • ISBN: 978-1-62937-735-3

Jumble® Drag Race
$9.95 • ISBN: 978-1-62937-483-3

Jumble® Ever After
$10.95 • ISBN: 978-1-62937-785-8

Jumble® Explorer
$9.95 • ISBN: 978-1-60078-854-3

Jumble® Explosion
$10.95 • ISBN: 978-1-60078-078-3

Jumble® Fever
$9.95 • ISBN: 978-1-57243-593-3

Jumble® Galaxy
$10.95 • ISBN: 978-1-60078-583-2

Jumble® Garden
$10.95 • ISBN: 978-1-62937-653-0

Jumble® Genius
$10.95 • ISBN: 978-1-57243-896-5

Jumble® Geography
$10.95 • ISBN: 978-1-62937-615-8

Jumble® Getaway
$10.95 • ISBN: 978-1-60078-547-4

Jumble® Gold
$10.95 • ISBN: 978-1-62937-354-6

Jumble® Health
$10.95 • ISBN: 978-1-63727-085-1

Jumble® Jackpot
$10.95 • ISBN: 978-1-57243-897-2

Jumble® Jailbreak
$9.95 • ISBN: 978-1-62937-002-6

Jumble® Jambalaya
$9.95 • ISBN: 978-1-60078-294-7

Jumble® Jitterbug
$10.95 • ISBN: 978-1-60078-584-9

Jumble® Journey
$10.95 • ISBN: 978-1-62937-549-6

Jumble® Jubilation
$10.95 • ISBN: 978-1-62937-784-1

Jumble® Jubilee
$10.95 • ISBN: 978-1-57243-231-4

Jumble® Juggernaut
$9.95 • ISBN: 978-1-60078-026-4

Jumble® Kingdom
$10.95 • ISBN: 978-1-62937-079-8

Jumble® Knockout
$9.95 • ISBN: 978-1-62937-078-1

Jumble® Madness
$10.95 • ISBN: 978-1-892049-24-7

Jumble® Magic
$9.95 • ISBN: 978-1-60078-795-9

Jumble® Mania
$10.95 • ISBN: 978-1-57243-697-8

Jumble® Marathon
$9.95 • ISBN: 978-1-60078-944-1

Jumble® Masterpiece
$10.95 • ISBN: 978-1-62937-916-6

Jumble® Neighbor
$10.95 • ISBN: 978-1-62937-845-9

Jumble® Parachute
$10.95 • ISBN: 978-1-62937-548-9

Jumble® Party
$10.95 • ISBN: 978-1-63727-008-0

Jumble® Safari
$9.95 • ISBN: 978-1-60078-675-4

Jumble® Sensation
$10.95 • ISBN: 978-1-60078-548-1

Jumble® Skyscraper
$10.95 • ISBN: 978-1-62937-869-5

Jumble® Symphony
$10.95 • ISBN: 978-1-62937-131-3

Jumble® Theater
$9.95 • ISBN: 978-1-62937-484-0

Jumble® Time Machine: 1972
$10.95 • ISBN: 978-1-63727-082-0

Jumble® Time Machine: 1993
$10.95 • ISBN: 978-1-63727-293-0

Jumble® Trouble
$10.95 • ISBN: 978-1-62937-917-3

Jumble® University
$10.95 • ISBN: 978-1-62937-001-9

Jumble® Unleashed
$10.95 • ISBN: 978-1-62937-844-2

Jumble® Vacation
$10.95 • ISBN: 978-1-60078-796-6

Jumble® Wedding
$9.95 • ISBN: 978-1-62937-307-2

Jumble® Workout
$10.95 • ISBN: 978-1-60078-943-4

Jump, Jive and Jumble®
$9.95 • ISBN: 978-1-60078-215-2

Lunar Jumble®
$9.95 • ISBN: 978-1-60078-853-6

Monster Jumble®
$10.95 • ISBN: 978-1-62937-213-6

Mystic Jumble®
$9.95 • ISBN: 978-1-62937-130-6

Rainy Day Jumble®
$10.95 • ISBN: 978-1-60078-352-4

Royal Jumble®
$10.95 • ISBN: 978-1-60078-738-6

Sports Jumble®
$10.95 • ISBN: 978-1-57243-113-3

Summer Fun Jumble®
$10.95 • ISBN: 978-1-57243-114-0

Touchdown Jumble®
$9.95 • ISBN: 978-1-62937-212-9

Oversize Jumble® Books

More than 500 puzzles!

Colossal Jumble®
$19.95 • ISBN: 978-1-57243-490-5

Jumbo Jumble®
$19.95 • ISBN: 978-1-57243-314-4

Jumble® Crosswords™

More than 175 puzzles!

Jumble® Crosswords™
$10.95 • ISBN: 978-1-57243-347-2